GARDENER'S
ABC

THE ESSENTIAL
GUIDE TO
GARDENING
TERMS

JOHN KELLY

WARD LOCK

First published in the UK 1995

by Ward Lock, Wellington House, 125 Strand
London WC2R 0BB

A Cassell Imprint

Distributed in the United States by Sterling Publishing Co., Inc.
387 Park Avenue South, New York, NY 10016-8810

Distributed in Australia by Capricorn Link (Australia) Pty Ltd
2/13 Carrington Road, Castle Hill NSW 2154

A British Library Cataloguing in Publication Data block for this book
may be obtained from the British Library

ISBN 0 7063 7372 3

Typeset by xheight Limited
Printed and bound in Great Britain by Hartnolls Ltd, Bodmin

FOREWORD

It can be an unpleasant experience to be surrounded by people enthusiastically using words you have never heard before and that you suspect you will never understand. Gardening can be like that. Get a gaggle of keen gardeners together and you may well be baffled by phrases such as 'You seen my parrot-beak? I need it to head back the water shoots?' or 'If I batter back I can create a space for my saxicoles'. Go to a flower show and hear a couple of boffins debating the number of papillae on the dorsal surface of the calyx and you will wonder what sort of world you are trying to join.

This small book does not begin to attempt to be comprehensive. It would have to be enormous to manage that. It will not turn you into a botanist and it may leave you at a loss when confronted by some ancient piece of gardening dialect, but it will set your feet well on the road to being able to understand the planty pundits and stand up to the botanical bores.

What is more, it should make your gardening more enjoyable by encouraging confidence and convincing you that, while gardening is an art and a craft with a little bit of science thrown in, it is highly accessible, great fun, deeply satisfying, and not difficult at all.

If you are an experienced gardener it is no use trying to fool me by saying that you know all that stuff already. Do you really know what a virus is? Have you begun to understand what is so damaging about applying excess fertilizer? Do you know a thrip from a thunderfly – or should you?

Just as I found, on the day I finished 'Z', that I did not know what an electrical relay was but had been using the term for years, I suspect that you will be quite keen to sneak away and sort out meristem, geotropism and corymb or even batter, broken and chipping. If you are, you will find more than mere definitions here. There are some useful practical hints as well.

You can keep this book on a bookshelf, in the potting shed or – and I honestly do not mind one bit – in the smallest room. The main thing is, make today the day you stopped bothering about gardening technicalities. They are only words, after all.

John Kelly
Pound Hill, Sussex and
The Borlin, Co. Cork, Ireland

ACCELERATOR see **activator**.

ACID RAIN rain containing dissolved sulphur dioxide and oxides of nitrogen from industrial processes. All rain is a very weak solution of carbonic acid, which is harmless. Acid rain, however, is harmful to plants, especially trees, and can cause die-back. Beware of attributing every dead twig to acid rain – you may be missing some other problem that can be treated. See **stag-headed**.

ACID SOIL a soil with no free lime and a **pH** of less than 6.5. Lime-hating plants such as rhododendrons, azaleas and camellias like growing in an acid soil.

ACTIVATOR a substance added to the compost heap to accelerate the rotting-down process. Activators are also known as accelerators and include substances such as **ammonium sulphate**, soil, and commercially formulated products.

ACUMINATE a term used to describe a leaf tip that tapers gradually and evenly to a long point.

ACUTE a term used to describe a leaf tip or base ending in a sharp point with nearly straight sides.

ADAPTATION (1) the process through which a plant passes in becoming used to a new type of environment, such as outdoors, having been under glass.

ADAPTATION (2) a change or modification in a plant that allows it to adapt to a new environment. This

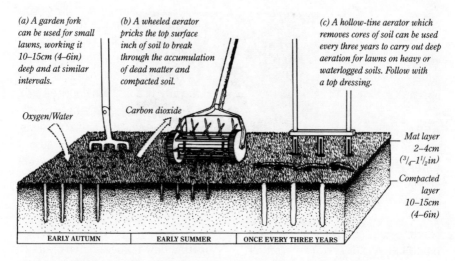

(a) A garden fork can be used for small lawns, working it 10–15cm (4–6in) deep and at similar intervals.

(b) A wheeled aerator pricks the top surface inch of soil to break through the accumulation of dead matter and compacted soil.

(c) A hollow-tine aerator which removes cores of soil can be used every three years to carry out deep aeration for lawns on heavy or waterlogged soils. Follow with a top dressing.

Oxygen/Water

Carbon dioxide

Mat layer 2–4cm ($^3/_4$–1$^1/_2$in)

Compacted layer 10–15cm (4–6in)

| EARLY AUTUMN | EARLY SUMMER | ONCE EVERY THREE YEARS |

AERATION for compacted soil. The idea is to create holes and slits which will allow the soil to 'breathe' and water to penetrate. (see Aerator, p7)

may take place genetically over time. For example, only the hardiest specimens of a species may survive in a cold climate, but they will survive to reproduce by seed and pass on their greater hardiness, thus producing an adapted population. Such characteristics are not acquired as a result of being in a more hostile environment but are inherent: individuals without them perish before they can reproduce.

ADPRESSED a term used to describe a plant part, such as a hair or a leaf, that lies flat against the stem or leaf to which it is attached. Examples are the hairs on the leaves of the pineapple broom

(*Cytisus battandieri*), which in the mass give them a silver-plated appearance, and the adult foliage of many cypresses (*Cupressus* and *Chamaecyparis*), in which the tiny, scale-like leaves are pressed tightly to the branchlets.

ADULT FOLIAGE some trees and shrubs have juvenile and adult leaves that are noticeably different. For example, in some conifers the juvenile leaves are long and needle shaped, whereas the adult leaves are small and scale-like. Young plants will have juvenile foliage but mature ones may bear adult or juvenile leaves or a mixture.

ADVENTITIOUS a term used to describe a shoot or root that arises in an unusual position. An adventitious root, for example, may appear growing from a leaf.

AERATING the process of allowing more air into the soil by digging or spiking to encourage an exchange of gases between soil and atmosphere. Plants will not thrive on a soil that is poorly aerated. Adequate aeration depends on making the soil **friable** and well drained. See **compaction**.

AERATOR a tool used to open up a lawn to the air by spiking or slitting. Hollow-tined forks are often used when aeration is desired without disturbing the smoothness of the turf, as in golf greens.

AERIAL ROOT a root that appears above soil or, in the case of aquatic plants, water level. Ivies, for example, produce aerial roots from the stems that act as anchors.

AEROBIC an airy environment in which oxygen is available.

AIR DRAINAGE it is not always appreciated that cold air behaves like cold water. It lies below warmer air, flows downhill and fills depres-

sions like water in a bath. A frost pocket is just such a depression. Frost pockets can also be formed, depending on the slope of the ground, if the flow of cold air is impeded by a wall or solid fence. This was one of the reasons why the walled gardens of large houses were often far less warm than might have been expected. Permeable barriers, such as trees, shrubs and hedges, allow the cold air to filter away.

AIR FROST this occurs where the temperature is 0°C (32°F) at a height of 1.2m (4ft) above the soil surface. See **ground frost**.

AIR LAYERING a method of propagating woody plants in which

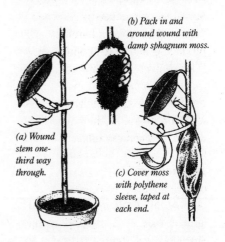

(b) Pack in and around wound with damp sphagnum moss.

(a) Wound stem one-third way through.

(c) Cover moss with polythene sleeve, taped at each end.

AIR LAYERING a rubber plant.

a stem or branch is induced to produce roots by enclosing a short section in a piece of a suitable medium, such as damp moss, and wrapping it in plastic sheet. It is frequently used for magnolias and rubber plants (*Ficus elastica*).

ALGAE primitive plants made up of one cell or chains or groups of cells. They contain **chlorophyll** and use light for making starches and sugars. Algae are responsible for making pond water green and slimy and they are very dangerous on paths, especially stone ones. Scrub flagstones and the like with domestic bleach, permanganate of potash, or scatter a copper sulphate powder sold in agricultural merchants as 'blue stone'. Control algae in ponds by stocking them with plenty of plants to shade the water and to compete with the algae for mineral salts.

ALIEN this term has a special meaning in botany and is used to refer to plants that have been introduced to a country and subsequently **naturalized**.

ALKALINE SOIL a soil with a **pH** greater than 7.0. Limy soils are alkaline, and chalk ones extremely so. Rhododendrons, azaleas, camellias and other lime-haters cannot be grown satisfactorily in them.

ALKALOIDS nitrogen-containing compounds produced by plants which often have strong effects on anything eating or nibbling them. This built-in defence mechanism has given us many poisons (strychnine, nicotine, colchicine), useful medicines (quinine, digitalin), as well as cocaine and morphine. A small amount of either of the alkaloids in the oleander (*Nerium oleander*), nerein and oleandrin, can kill several people, so whatever you do, do not use their stems for kebab skewers. It has been known.

ALPINE botanically, a plant that occurs between the tree line and the permanent snow line is described as an alpine. In the Arctic this can be fairly close to sea level but it is generally a mountain zone. However, in gardening alpines are plants that are suitable for the **rock garden**.

ALPINE HOUSE an airy, unheated greenhouse, often with open sides to provide plenty of ventilation.

ALTERNATE a term used to describe leaves that are arranged alternately on a stem, one arising from each node, as distinct from **opposite** leaves in pairs. You may wonder why this should be significant. From a gardening point of view it is not at all important but it is a good starting point in plant identification.

AMMONIUM NITRATE a fertilizer containing 34 per cent combined nitrogen. It makes the soil acid after a few applications and is best applied as nitro-chalk, in which it is mixed with lime to balance the acidity.

AMMONIUM SULPHATE also known as sulphate of ammonia, a nitrogen fertilizer not much used as such today because of its acidifying effect. It is, however, very useful as a killer of weeds in lawns when used in the mixture known as **lawn sand**. It is also a good compost **activator**. Ammonium sulphate should not be confused with ammonium sulphamate, which is used to kill stumps by inserting it between slips of bark and the wood at the cut edge of the stump.

ANGIOSPERM a member of the group of plants that flower and produce seeds enclosed in a **fruit**. See **gymnosperm**.

ANNUAL a plant that germinates, grows, flowers, sets seed and then dies all within one growing season.

ANNUAL RING in woody plants a layer of wood called **xylem** is laid down every growing season. It is in the form of a cylinder and therefore when the tree is cut down the layers show as annual rings in the cross section. They vary in width according to how favourable each year was for growth, and by counting them you can establish the age of the tree. Living trees can be aged by boring their trunks with an auger and counting the stripes on the resultant core sample.

ANNUAL SHOOT the shoot produced by a herbaceous perennial or a bulb is known as an annual shoot because it persists for only one growing season

ANTHER the part of the flower that bears the pollen. It is the upper part of the **stamen**.

ANTHRACNOSE a group of fungal diseases causing dark spots on leaves, stems and fruits.

APHIDS a large group of sap-feeding insects, including greenfly, blackfly and many other garden pests.

APICAL BUD the bud at the tip of a stem.

APICAL DOMINANCE a natural process in which hormones produced by an **apical bud** inhibit the growth of the lateral (side-shoot) buds. If apical dominance is counteracted by removal of the apical bud, side-shoots are encouraged and the plant becomes bushy. This is the principle behind '**pinching-out**' young plants.

APICULATE a term used to describe a leaf tip that has a short, sharp but not rigid point at the end even though the leaf itself is fairly blunt.

AQUATIC any plant that grows in water, either partially or completely submerged. Depending on where they grow, aquatics can be deep-water plants, such as water lilies (*Nymphaea*), floating plants, such as fairy moss (*Azolla caroliniana*), submerged plants, such as Canadian pond weed (*Elodea canadensis*) or marginals, such as water mint (*Mentha aquatica*).

ARBORETUM a large garden or park devoted to a collection of trees and shrubs. They are usually planted both to look pleasant and to provide material for study, and thus appeal to you and me as well as botanists and horticulturalists.

ARBORICULTURE the science, practice and art of growing and caring for trees.

ARBORICULTURIST an expert on trees and tree care. Remember that this term is not synonymous with tree surgeon. A **tree surgeon** may or may not be an arboriculturist. Beware of cowboys, masquerading as tree surgeons or arboriculturists, who are a danger to you and your trees.

ARBOUR any shady, sheltered place made deliberately to provide privacy. It is usually made by erecting trellis or other timber-work and growing plants on it, but you can also make an arbour solely with plants. An arbour can be made as a roofed recess in a tall hedge or by growing a circle of trees such as hornbeams (*Carpinus*) and drawing their tops together when they are still young and pliable. A bower is much the same thing but the word does not imply quite as strongly the notion of overhead cover.

ARMILLARIA ROOT ROT see **honey fungus**.

AROID a term applied to any plant belonging to the arum family. Their 'flowers' (strictly **inflorescences**) are made up of a finger-like **spadix** within a **spathe** that looks something like a paper cone. Lords-and-ladies (*Arum maculatum*) is an aroid.

AUXINS a group of plant hormones that regulate many aspects of plant growth. Among the functions they govern are **apical dominance** and the intitiation of roots. They are used in hormone rooting powders and liquids for propagation and can also be formulated as herbi-

cides, killing weeds by making them outgrow themselves.

AXE (WOODSMAN'S) a tool neither owned nor used by sensible gardeners. Buy a cross-axe for usefulness and safety and a stout pruning saw. The woodsman's axe is safe in the hands of a woodsman and nobody else. To use a blunt axe is about as sensible as putting your legs in the path of a truck. See **mattock**.

AXIL the upper angle between a leaf or stem and the stem from which it arises.

AXILLARY BUD a bud arising from an **axil**. Not to be confused with auxiliary, meaning something additional or subsidiary.

BACK-CROSS a cross made between a **hybrid** and one of its parents. Back-crosses are often made to strengthen genetic tendencies such as **hardiness**, long stems, freedom of flowering, resistance to disease and so on.

BACTERIA usually one-celled, microscopic organisms without chlorophyll – neither plants nor animals. Most bacteria in the garden are beneficial, bringing about the decay process indispensable to healthy soil, but some give rise to plant diseases, which are often hard to cure.

BAG FERTILIZER concentrated artificial fertilizer supplied in bags. Professionals use it more than amateurs, as they apply larger quantities of fertilizer.

BALANCED FERTILIZER a fertilizer that contains equal proportions of usable nitrogen, phosphate and potassium. See **NPK**.

BALLED term used to describe field-grown trees and shrubs whose roots are in a ball of soil wrapped in hessian or plastic netting. If plastic, the wrapping must be removed when planting and many gardeners prefer to remove hessian as well.

BARE-ROOT (OR BARE-ROOTED) term used to describe plants that are field-grown and lifted without any soil round their roots. **Herbaceous perennials**, roses and trees are often supplied bare-rooted for planting in autumn or winter.

BARK (SHREDDED) also known as forest bark, it comes mostly from conifers and makes a reasonable substitute for peat in composts and an excellent and decorative garden **mulch**. Make sure you buy 'composted' bark, otherwise its breakdown will rob the soil of nitrogen. Alternatively, stack it to rot down for a year.

BARK BEETLES insects whose **larvae** live in or under the bark of woody plants. The worst of them as a pest is the elm bark beetle, which carries a fungus that causes Dutch elm disease.

BASAL ROT a fungal disease of bulbs causing rotting at the base of crocus, narcissus and lily bulbs. Affected bulbs should be destroyed.

BASE FERTILIZER a fertilizer that is mixed into compost according to a set formula, as in the **John Innes composts**.

BATTER the slight backward slope of a rock wall, soil bank or retaining wall, but particularly the slope of the sides of a clipped hedge. When building a rock garden, successive layers of rocks are 'battered back' from one another.

BED an area of soil specifically prepared and maintained for intensive planting. It is approachable from all sides (as distinct from a **border**) and can be cut out of a lawn, set among paving or gravel or even raised within walls or other surrounds. See **island bed**, **raised bed**.

BED SYSTEM there are several versions of this method of growing vegetables but all of them are based on the principle of constructing narrow beds that can be cultivated from paths between them. The benefits are that the soil is not trodden down by your feet, allowing it to become raised and well **aerated**, and the beds are easily covered with **cloches** and other protective materials, allowing earlier crops. Bed systems are especially useful on heavy soils.

BEDDING a planting consisting of temporary plants, often in place for only one season or part of a season, used in fairly large numbers. Bedding can be formal or informal. Easily propagated annuals, biennials and bulbs are the groups of plants normally used, but tender perennials such as argyranthemums and shrubs such as fuchsias can be bedded out by taking cuttings annually to produce large numbers of plants that can be overwintered under glass.

BELL JAR a glass, bell-shaped vessel used with the open end downwards to protect crops. They are thought of as impossibly old-fashioned but are worth their weight in gold. See **cloche**.

BELT a strip of trees or shrubs, usually planted for shelter from wind. In classical form (as used on country estates where money and space are no object and overkill is the general rule) it should be one chain (i.e. 20m/22 yards) deep! It is, for all that, a mistake to rely on too shallow a shelter belt.

BELVEDERE from the Italian *bel vedere*, a beautiful view. In a garden a belvedere is a summer house with a vista, but it has to be quite a view. To call it a belvedere when it looks over the delivery dock of a supermarket is a little pretentious. A belvedere need not have a roof. After all, who wants to look at the view when it is raining?

BENDING a process by which the branches of fruit trees and some ornamental shrubs are made more productive by training them near horizontally to restrict their sap flow. The branches of fruit trees may be lowered by **guying** them down, with or without weights.

Climbing and rambling roses are sometimes grown spirally on pyramids of canes so that their branches are only just enough above horizontal to climb the pyramid. This greatly increases flowering. Bourbon and other repeat-flowering old roses are often trained on ropes or pegged down to the ground for the same purpose.

BESOM a broom made with twigs, usually, but not always of birch or hazel, tied in a bundle to a long handle. It is ideal for sweeping up leaves and better than anything else for removing debris from gravel paths.

BICOLOR a term used to describe a flower made up of two colours.

BIENNIAL a plant that germinates and makes all its growth in one year, then flowers, sets seed and dies in the second.

BIFURCATE a term used to describe something that is forked in two or y-shaped.

BIG BUD a disease of blackcurrants characterized by the swelling of the dormant buds in late winter. It is caused by infestation by a tiny **mite**, which also carries with it the virus causing **reversion**.

BIGENERIC HYBRID a cross between two different genera. It is denoted by an x before the name. For example, x *Phyllothamnus* is a bigeneric hybrid between *Phyllodoce* and *Rhodothamnus*. Such hybrids are not as unusual among plants as they are among animals and may occur either naturally or in culti-vation. As with animals, however, they are usually sterile (**mules**).

BILLHOOK a wide-bladed, heavy knife with a hook near the tip. It is used in making agricultural hedges and for **brashing**.

BINOMIAL SYSTEM the system of **naming of plants** developed in the eighteenth century by the Swedish botanist, Carl Linnaeus. All plant species are given a latinized name, based on two words: the name of the genus (e.g. *Skimmia*) followed by the name of the species (e.g. *japonica*), to give a binomial (two-part name) (*Skimmia japonica*). See **Latin names**.

BIOLOGICAL CONTROL an increasingly popular method of pest control in which other living organisms are used to kill the pests

or interfere with their life-cycles so that they die out. Victorian gardeners often kept a toad in the greenhouse to deal with insects. Today, greenhouse whitefly can be controlled by hanging bits of card or leaf carrying the larvae of a tiny parasitic wasp called *Encarsia formosa* on affected plants.

BISEXUAL a term used to describe plants whose flowers have both male and female organs. It is not 'either or' but 'both and'.

BLACK SPOT a very common disease of roses, causing black spots on the leaves and ultimately the loss of all leaves. It is very infectious, so affected plants should be sprayed and any diseased leaves removed and burned straight away. Danger of black spot can be reduced by keeping roses well fed and healthy or by growing **resistant** varieties.

BLADE the flattened part of a leaf as opposed to the stalk or **petiole**.

BLANCHING if you exclude the light from green plants they will lose their green pigment. Do this to the entire plant and it will die, but if you keep the light away from parts of some vegetables it removes bitterness and makes them much more palatable. Vegetables that are deliberately blanched include celery, chicory, leeks and seakale. **Earthing-up** potatoes is a method of blanching; tubers exposed to the light turn green and become poisonous.

BLEEDING you may be warned not to prune a tree or shrub during the growing season because it will 'bleed'. Bleeding in this context is an unremitting flow of sap from the cut surface of a branch or shoot. Notorious bleeders are grape vines and maples and they should be pruned only in winter when the sap is not rising. In the old days a pinch of bonfire ash was applied to cut surfaces to stop bleeding. It seemed to work.

BLIGHT a fungal disease affect-ing tomatoes and potatoes that rapidly destroys plants. It can be controlled by spraying with **Bordeaux mixture**.

BLIND a term used to describe a plant with a damaged or destroyed growing point. It applies particu-larly to bulbs. Bulbs growing in grass will come up blind (and will not flower) if the grass was mown in the previous year less than

seven weeks after flowering ceased. A true palm will be rendered blind if its growing point is damaged, as it has only the one.

BLOOM (1) a flower.

BLOOM (2) a powdery or waxy coating, usually white but quite often blue, on stems, leaves or fruits. *Rubus cockburnianus* has strikingly white-bloomed stems; *Zenobia pulverulenta* has bloomy leaves, and many kinds of plum are covered with a powdery bloom. A bloom is usually easily washed or rubbed off. See **glaucous**, **pruinose**.

BLUE STONE see **copper sulphate**.

BLUEING COMPOUND some hydrangeas can be persuaded to produce blue flowers. This happens naturally in **acid soils** in which there is an adequate supply of free aluminium but in slightly **alkaline soils**, which render aluminium unobtainable to the plants, blueing compounds need to be added to change the colour of flowers that would otherwise be pink. It does not work with really alkaline soils.

BOG GARDEN a part of the garden devoted to plants that prefer boggy conditions. Bog plants do not necessarily tolerate bad drainage and stagnancy; a slow flow of water through a peaty, marshy soil suits them. You can make a bog garden either by extending the margin of a pond or by using a pond liner beneath the soil to hold moisture. Many of the plants that enjoy a permanently wet soil are among the most beautiful of all, for example, candelabra primulas or the Siberian iris (*Iris sibirica*).

BOLE the main stem of a tree: the **trunk**, but especially that part of it below the first branch.

BOLTING a term used to describe the production of an unwanted flower stem, especially in vegetables. Lettuces, in particular, are prone to bolting as a response to overcrowding or shortage of water. Once bolted, the plant will be bitter and useless for eating.

BONSAI a fairly misunderstood Japanese art of dwarfing plants, mainly trees and shrubs, by special techniques involving **root pruning**, **pinching-out** and training branches and stems.

BORDEAUX MIXTURE a useful fungicide consisting of a mixture

Constructing an independent **BOG GARDEN**.

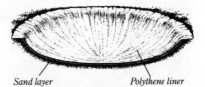

Sand layer *Polythene liner*

(a) A PVC or polythene liner used in a sand-lined excavation.

Layer of soil covers liner at edges

(b) Fill with a moisture-retentive soil and plant

of copper sulphate and hydrated lime developed many years ago to deal with fungal disease in the vineyards of Bordeaux. It is still used against potato blight.

BORDER a piece of cultivated soil, usually much longer than it is deep, one side of which consists of a wall, hedge or fence. It need not have a constant width and its free edge can be as curved as you wish. See **bed**.

BORROWED LANDSCAPE a technique whereby features outside the garden are made to appear continuous with it. The Japanese are thought to have originated it.

BOTANIC GARDEN contrary to the belief in some quarters, you

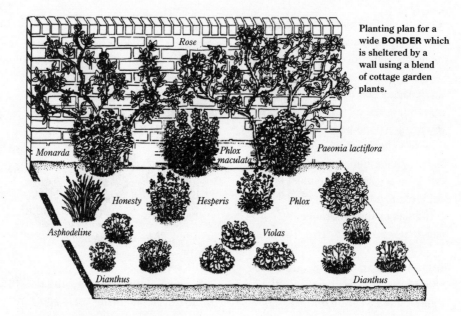

Planting plan for a wide **BORDER** which is sheltered by a wall using a blend of cottage garden plants.

Rose

Monarda   Phlox maculata   Paeonia lactiflora

Honesty   Hesperis   Phlox

Asphodeline   Violas

Dianthus   Dianthus

cannot just call your garden a botanic garden. It must be specifically designed for study and what is more it must contribute to it. It may be formal, as in the Clusius Botanic Garden at Leyden in Holland or relatively informal, as in the Edinburgh Botanic Garden, but the academic purpose is still evident.

BOTANICAL NAMES see **Latin names, naming of plants**.

BOTRYTIS also known as grey mould, this extremely common disease causes a fluffy, greyish mould on the stems and fruit of many plants including straw-berries, lettuces and tomatoes. It thrives in damp, cold conditions.

BOTTLE GARDEN a self-generating garden in a bottle or other closed glass case, in which plants live with very little need for water or food. See **Wardian case**.

BOTTOM HEAT germination of seeds or the rooting of cuttings is often speeded up or initiated early by the application of heat from beneath. Bottom heat can be supplied by a heated **propagator** or soil-warming cables.

BOWER see **arbour**.

BRACKET FUNGI a family of fungi that grow on the trunk and branches of trees. Some are harmless but some will damage the tree. If in doubt, call in an expert.

BRACT a modified leaf that acts as a protection for an **inflorescence**, bud or shoot and is usually found at its base. A bract can be very small and scale-like or large and highly ornamental, as in *Bougainvillea* and some *Cornus* species.

BRACTEOLE a small bract from which a flower or flowers may arise, as in snowdrops (*Galanthus*).

BRANCHLET not a twee term but a precise one, meaning the shoots of the current year and the year before.

BRASHING a process in which the branches of young trees are removed up to a height that will allow people to walk unimpeded. It is done with a **billhook** in forestry but is better carried out with **pruning tools** in the garden.

BROAD-LEAVED a loose term used to describe trees whose leaves are broad and flat compared with those of conifers, which are narrow and needle-like. Like all distinctions in nature, it is fuzzy-edged. Some conifers (e.g. the willow-leaf podocarp, *Podocarpus salignus*) and some broad-leaved trees (e.g. many willows and a few eucalyptus) have leaves that are very similar in appearance.

BROADCAST a method of sowing seed in which it is scattered rather than sown in rows or patterns.

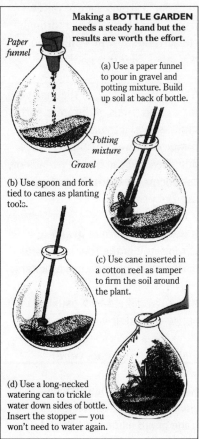

Making a **BOTTLE GARDEN** needs a steady hand but the results are worth the effort.

Paper funnel

(a) Use a paper funnel to pour in gravel and potting mixture. Build up soil at back of bottle.

Potting mixture

Gravel

(b) Use spoon and fork tied to canes as planting tools.

(c) Use cane inserted in a cotton reel as tamper to firm the soil around the plant.

(d) Use a long-necked watering can to trickle water down sides of bottle. Insert the stopper — you won't need to water again.

BROKEN a term used to describe flowers in which the colours have disintegrated into stripes, flashes and splashes. It applies especially to tulips, in which the broken effect is due to viruses and was highly sought after many years ago. Broken tulips are enjoying a new wave of popularity.

BUBBLE FOUNTAIN a type of fountain in which a jet of water rises without great force through cobbles, the hole in a millstone, or any other similar device.

BUD a shoot or organ that has yet to develop. Buds of different sorts may develop into individual flowers, flower clusters, leaf clusters or branches and can be at the ends of the shoots (**terminal**) or at a joint (**axillary**).

BUDDING a form of **grafting** used extensively in the rose trade and hardly at all by amateur gardeners.

BULB a modified bud, usually below ground. It is a short, fleshy stem and acts as a storage organ. See **corm**, **rhizome**, **tuber**.

BULB FIBRE fibrous substance, now sold almost entirely under trade brand names, in which bulbs can be grown for a season in bowls without drainage holes.

BULB FRAME a glass structure used by bulb experts in which to grow bulbs that need a completely dry dormant spell.

BULB PLANTER a tool consisting of a slightly tapered cylindrical blade which is used to remove a plug of soil just the right depth for planting bulbs. It is an unnecessary tool if you know how to use a trowel.

BULBIL a minute bulb growing in the axil of a leaf, among the flowers or, as in some lilies, on the stem.

BULBLET another term for **bulbil**, but usually applied to the tiny bulbs produced by plants such as *Iris danfordiae*, in which all that appears to be left after a year's growth and flowering are minute organs like so many grains of wheat.

BULBOUS (1) a term used to describe a stem that is swollen at the base.

BULBOUS (2) a term applied to a plant that has a bulb.

BULK a term used to distinguish quantity by volume as opposed

GARDENER'S ABC

to weight. For example, a good cuttings compost is 50/50 moss peat and sharp sand by bulk. This value by weight would be useless.

BULKY a term applied to manures that do not contain very much plant food per unit of volume. Strawy manures are bulky or high on bulk before they have properly rotted down.

BULLATE a term used to describe a leaf with a blistered or puckered surface.

BUSH simple in general; less so in gardening. A bush may be a small shrub with many branching stems, fruit such as gooseberries and currants, a dwarfed fruit tree, or a tomato variety that grows to a relatively low height and then stops of its own accord.

CALCAREOUS SOIL an **alkaline soil** containing calcium carbonate (chalk, limestone) or magnesium carbonate (dolomitic limestone).

CALCICOLE a plant that thrives best on a calcareous soil, such as many dianthus and campanulas.

CALCIFUGE a plant that will not grow in calcareous soils. Such plants are often called lime-haters. Rhododendrons and camellias are calcifuges.

CALCIUM one of the **macro-nutrients** (i.e. substances required in quite large amounts) needed by plants. Deficiency is rare in a well-managed garden.

CALCIUM CARBONATE chalk and limestone.

CALCIUM HYDROXIDE hydrated lime, used for liming soils to raise their **pH**.

CALCIUM OXIDE quicklime. A dangerous substance best kept out of the garden.

CALLUS when a plant has been wounded, a corky type of tissue builds up to heal the wound. This is called callus. It forms at the wounded surface of a **cutting** and the new roots are formed from it.

CALYX the outermost part of a flower, consisting of **sepals** that enclose and protect the flower bud as it develops.

CAMBIUM a layer of living cells, immediately below the bark, producing material that adds to the thickness of the stem.

CANE FRUITS a group of fruits, such as raspberries and logan-berries, that are produced on cane-like stems.

CANKER a number of diseases that cause sunken patches of dead tissue on stems, often oozing a sticky substance. Cankers often attack roses and fruit trees. Affected stems and small branches should be cut off and burnt as soon as the disease is noticed.

CAPILLARY MATTING a special matting, along and through which water percolates by capillary action and on which pots are stood so that water rises from the matting into the compost. It is very labour-saving in the greenhouse and is increasingly used for standing-out beds in the open.

CAPPING the formation of a layer on the surface of the soil through which water cannot easily pass. On light soils and silts it can be caused by the action of rain drops, and artificial irrigation can give rise to capping on almost any soil if it is mismanaged. Capping often follows if a sprinkler is left running for too

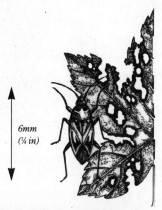

6mm
(¼ in)

CAPSID BUGS may be hard to spot but the tattered holes in the somewhat distorted foliage are very characteristic.

long. A capped soil reduces the amount of water and air that can pass through its surface and also makes it difficult for seedlings to emerge.

CAPSID BUGS sap-sucking insects related to **aphids** that can cause considerable damage to leaves, stems, flowers and fruit. They are not often spotted because they are very small but they produce characteristic damage in the form of tiny holes that become bigger as the leaf grows and distorted foliage. They are usually controlled by the use of **systemic** insecticides.

CARNIVOROUS PLANTS see **insectivorous plants**.

CARPET BEDDING a special way of **bedding** with small foliage plants so as to make designs or even pictures on the ground. The soil is firmed gently and then the design is drawn by releasing a slow stream of sand from the hand or, in the case of geometrical figures such as circles, by using sticks and string. It is used almost exclusively in public gardens.

CATCH CROP during the time that elapses between harvesting a main crop from a patch of ground and sowing the next, a very fast-growing crop may be sown and harvested. Radishes are an example of a catch crop.

CAUDEX a swollen stem-base, found usually in succulents. The most extreme example is the baobab tree of the tropics.

CELLULOSE the main component of the walls of plant cells.

CHAINSAW a saw that cuts by means of a power-driven chain. Chainsaws should never be used by anyone, professional or amateur, unless they have attended an approved training course and are wearing the full complement of protective equipment – hard helmet, ear defenders, goggles or visor, Kevlar bib and brace overalls, Kevlar gloves and reinforced boots.

CHALK soft, white, calcium carbonate limestone. It is chemically different from 'school' chalk. It was laid down in the Cretaceous Period, 140 million years ago, by the deposition of the shells of minute organisms in very shallow, warm seas. The soil that lies above it is often very shallow and easily becomes dry and hot. Gardens on chalk are restricted in the variety of plants that can be grown in them.

CHECK a period during which the growth of a plant stops when it should not. Anything – such as drought, a draught, or becoming **pot-bound** – that causes a plant to 'take a check' is to be avoided.

CHELATE in alkaline soils, some elements essential to plants may become locked into compounds that cannot be absorbed by the roots. This applies particularly to iron, which is needed to make **chlorophyll** – the green pigment in plants. In a chelate the essential element is held in a form that cannot react with the soil, thus making it available to the plants. Sequestrene is a well-known chelate of iron. See **chlorosis**.

CHESHUNT COMPOUND a copper fungicide used to prevent **damping-off**.

CHIMERA a plant in which tissues of two distinct genera co-exist. It may happen naturally or in grafting and is denoted by a + sign. Examples of graft chimeras are + *Laburnocytisus* (laburnum + broom) and + *Crataegomespilus* (hawthorn + medlar). It is not the same as the parasitic type of association of tissues, which is harmful, as when mistletoe grows on an apple tree.

CHIPPING (1) the practice of abrading or puncturing seeds with hard coats in order to let water in so that they will germinate more quickly. Often used with sweet pea (*Lathyrus odoratus*) seeds.

CHIPPING (2) the method of propagating bulbs by slicing them with a knife.

CHITTING the practice of laying seed potatoes out to sprout before planting. The term is also applied to processes used to encourage seeds to germinate before they are sown. For example, Russell lupins (*Lupinus* cultivars) are often germinated on moist blotting paper before being sown in compost. Not to be confused with **chipping**.

CHLOROPHYLL green plant pigment, containing iron and magnesium. It is central to **photosynthesis**, the process whereby plants use the energy of light to convert carbon dioxide and water into plant tissue.

CHLOROSIS deficiency disease characterized by yellowing of the leaves. The usual cause is un-availability of iron or magnesium, often due to lime in the soil, preventing production of suffi-cient chlorophyll. 'Lime-haters' are especially prone to chlorosis. See **alkaline soil**, **chelate**.

CHROMOSOME a body within the cell nucleus, consisting of DNA and carrying the genetic code for the organism. The number of chromosomes in a cell of a plant is useful to botanists for purposes of identification. Many gardeners silently curse the advent of chromosome science, as the knowledge it has brought has led to the reclassification of many species and changes of familiar names. We must, however, accept that the advance of science is a tide with which we must swim.

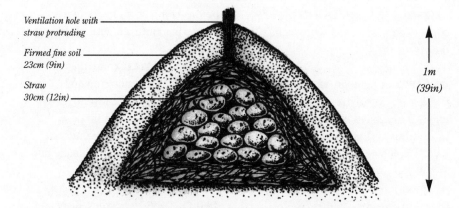

Ventilation hole with
straw protruding

Firmed fine soil
23cm (9in)

Straw
30cm (12in)

1m
(39in)

CLAMPING is a useful method of storage when you have a glut of potatoes, carrots or turnips. Always ensure that only completely healthy and unmarked tubers are stored and do not use any that have been damaged on lifting.

CILIATE a term used to describe a leaf, petal or stem with a margin of fine hairs.

CLAMP not a method of enforcing parking regulations but a method of storing root vegetables, especially potatoes, in the open in winter. The vegetables are placed in layers with soil and straw until a large mound is made. A clamp will be inefficient if it is small.

CLASSIFICATION the scientists' division of the plant kingdom into categories. All the gardener needs to know is that there are many plant **families** divided into related genera (the plural of **genus**), each of which comprises one or many **species**. The species are further divided into subspecies, varieties and forms. See **bionomial system, Latin names, naming of plants.**

CLAY a very stiff, difficult soil. Its main characteristic is invisible to the eye and is the extremely small size of the soil particles, less than 0.002mm. This is the direct cause of the way that clays behave in retaining water and the reason for the fact that they are so hard to work. Clays are highly fertile but are sticky in the wet and bone hard in the dry. They are late to start in spring and early to finish in autumn and swiftly lose their structure if worked when wet. Once improved by the addition of large amounts of **bulky** organic matter, however, a clay soil is among the very best. The addition of grit and sand is not such a good idea; to be effective, such large amounts are involved that the soil becomes hungry and thirsty.

CLOCHE originally meaning a **bell jar**, now a term applied to any small structure made of glass or plastic and wire, placed over crops to make them mature early. Nowadays tunnel cloches are available and are efficient, inexpensive and easy to handle.

CLONES genetically identical plants, produced by asexual propagation from a single parent.

CLUBROOT a soil-borne fungal disease of plants of the family Cruciferae, especially troublesome in brassicas (cabbages and their relatives). Clubroot causes the roots to swell and stop functioning. It thrives in poorly drained, acid soils and so can be prevented to a certain extent by adequate liming. However, there is no effective cure so it is best to avoid growing susceptible crops in soil known to be infected.

CLUSTER a term used loosely by gardeners for a group of flowers or sometimes leaves. Botanists distinguish between **racemes**, **corymbs**, **panicles**, **umbels** and so on – all describing different arrangements of flowers in an **inflorescence**. Where the distinctions should be made, 'cluster' is inadequate, but its general use in gardening is wrong only among the pedantic.

CODLING MOTH a pest mainly of apples but also pears. The females lay eggs on the developing apples and the maggots eat their way into the fruit. Control is usually by spraying with insecticide, although **pheromone traps** are increasingly used these days.

The swollen root characteristic of **CLUBROOT**.

COIR, COCONUT FIBRE a waste product of the copra industry, now in vogue as an environmentally friendly substitute for peat for use in seed and cuttings compost and as a **soil conditioner**. See **peat**.

COLD FRAME a framework holding panes or panels of glass or clear, rigid plastic, resting on or hinged to a sloping box. The frame and box may be made of any suitable materials. It is used for propagating plants, storing plants over winter, or as a step in hardening-off plants that have been in the greenhouse. Frames may also be heated, usually with soil-heating cables.

COLD GREENHOUSE a glass-house that is not heated. See **cool house**, **warm house**.

COLOUR BORDER an ambiguous term but one usually applied to borders in which flowers of one colour are grown. It takes a very skilful gardener to make a success-ful one and people may be tempted, on seeing it, to ask if it was worth the bother. White borders (or white gardens) swiftly become brown bor-ders unless there is an unceasing programme of dead-heading, prefer-ably carried out by someone else.

COMMON NAMES there are deep bogs ahead for gardeners who insist on using common names to the exclusion of scientific (Latin) names. The most important point is that common names are not common to different languages or across inter-national boundaries whereas **Latin names** are. As for those who find Latin names too long and difficult to pronounce, they may find that they prefer *Chiranthodendron penta-dactylon*, even though it has 29 letters, to its Mexican common name of macpalxochitlquahuitl, which has a mere 21!

COMPACTION treading on a wet soil, overworking soils or allowing too much traffic in feet or machin-ery causes the deterioration of soil structure and the exclusion of air. It is a much more frequent cause of trouble than most people think and is often the true cause of problems in plants that are blamed on diseases. See **aerating**.

COMPANION PLANTING a practice, especially popular among organic gardeners, of growing as close neighbours plants that are supposed to increase the well-being of one another. It is used largely in an attempt to control pests, as in the planting of marigolds (*Tagetes* and

Calendula) near tomatoes to control aphids. The theory is that the bright flowers of the marigolds attract hoverflies whose **larvae** eat aphids. I have seen little scientific evidence that it actually works and one should perhaps neither scoff nor necessarily follow suit.

COMPOST (I) an amorphous, black, friable substance high in **humus** and plant nutrients made by decomposing any plant or animal matter, including kitchen waste but not weeds with perennial roots, in a **compost heap**. It is incorporated in the soil to improve texture and add nutrients.

COMPOST (2) potting, cutting or sowing mixture made from soil, peat or peat substitute with added materials such as sand and fertilizers.

COMPOST HEAP a mass of organic material collected together to rot down to form compost.

CONCENTRATED FERTILIZER not a loose term but one specifying a fertilizer consisting of at least 30 per cent nitrogen, phosphorus and potassium (**NPK**).

CONDITIONER see **soil conditioner**.

CONSERVATORY at one time 'conservatory' and 'greenhouse' were synonyms. Later, the greenhouse became thought of more as a production unit, while the conservatory was a place in which to grow more mature plants and to enjoy and study them. Nowadays, as the uses of greenhouses widen to include displays of plants as well as their production, the term conservatory is generally reserved for a construction that is attached to one wall of a house.

CONTACT INSECTICIDE a chemical that kills insects on contact, as opposed to one that is absorbed by the plant and kills insects that ingest the sap. See **systemic**.

CONTAINER any vessel in which plants can be grown. It has two shades of meaning: (a) tubs, urns and other vessels in which plants are grown in the garden or conservatory and (b) the pots, bags and tins in which plants are grown in a nursery.

CONTAINER-GROWN an honest term in most nurseries, where plants are grown in containers so that they can be handled with ease and planted out at any time of

Suggestions for planting up a large **CONTAINER** or tub for spring colour.

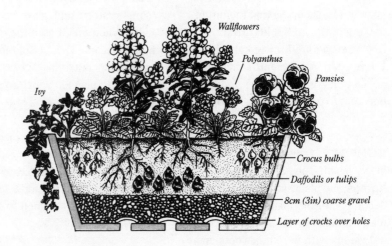

Wallflowers

Polyanthus

Pansies

Ivy

Crocus bulbs
Daffodils or tulips
8cm (3in) coarse gravel
Layer of crocks over holes

year. Unfortunately it is sometimes dishonestly applied to field-grown plants that have been forced into containers, a process that produces larger plants more quickly. It does not, however, provide gardeners with decent goods.

CONTINUOUS LAYERING see **French layering**.

COOL HOUSE a greenhouse in which the minimum winter temperature is maintained at 7°C (45°F).

COPPER SULPHATE a compound with two principal uses. When mixed with lime to make Bordeaux mixture, it is still the treatment of choice for preventing potato blight.

It is also the best way of treating slippery algae on paving and paths, bought as a powder known as 'blue stone' and scattered.

COPPICING the regular cutting down of young growths from the bases of trees, especially hazel and chestnut, so that the vertical shoots can be harvested for fences, hurdles and so on. While the term is hardly ever applied in gardening, it is nevertheless coppicing when you obey the instruction to 'cut back hard in early spring' such shrubs as *Cornus alba* 'Sibirica', *Salix daphnoides* and *Acer* 'Brilliantissimum'.

CORAL SPOT a fungus that produces coral-coloured pustules on wood. It can occur on many trees and shrubs, especially acers and magnolias. Infected wood should be removed and burnt.

CORDATE a term used to describe a heart-shaped leaf or bract.

CORDON a method of training fruit trees to form a single stem with no major spreading branches. It is also used for sweetpeas grown for show.

CORM a storage organ consisting of a solid, swollen stem covered by membraneous sheaths. Each corm lasts for one year, after which it is supplanted by a new one. Gladioli and crocuses grow from corms.

COROLLA often conspicuous part of the flower consisting of the petals.

CORYMB a flat-topped or slightly domed flower cluster or **inflorescence** in which the outer flowers open first.

COTTAGE GARDEN a colourful, informal, small garden, in which plants of all kinds – ornamental and productive – grow without being segregated. It is, of course, a romantic concept, originally dreamt up by the Victorians, that has little to do with the reality of the lives of people

who lived in cottages. However, it is now a popular form of garden suitable for town or country. Traditional cottage garden plants include hollyhocks (*Alcea rosea*), lavender (*Lavandula*), roses, honeysuckle (*Lonicera*), delphiniums, lupins (*Lupinus*) and many more.

COTYLEDON a seed leaf. Most plants have two (**dicotyledons**), but others, including most bulbous plants and grasses, have only one (**monocotyledons**). Some conifers have several in a whorl.

CREEPER strictly speaking a plant that grows horizontally over the ground and roots as it goes. Climbers are, however, often referred to as creepers (e.g. Virginia creeper, *Parthenocissus quinquefolia*).

CRISPED a term used mainly when describing fern fronds, meaning irregularly curled.

CROCKS bits of broken pot placed as a 'drainage' layer in the bottom of pots. Nowadays it is realized that a well-drained compost should not need crocks, and that unnecessary crocks merely take up space that could be occupied by nutritious compost. The trickiest alpines, including dionysias and raoulias, need only

31

one slightly curved crock over the drainage hole of their clay pot.

CROSS-POLLINATION the transfer of pollen from the flower of one plant to that of another, resulting in cross-fertilization, as opposed to self-pollination, in which pollen is transferred to another flower of the same plant.

CROWN (1) the head of branches of a tree.

CROWN (2) in herbaceous perennials, the crown is the area where the shoots arise from the rootstock. One plant may have several crowns and their separation allows their propagation. See **division**.

CULTIVAR a variety that originated in cultivation – a cultivated variety. Cultivar names are given in single quote marks with a capital first letter and are usually but not always in a modern language rather than Latin. For example, *Lithodora diffusa* 'Heavenly Blue'. If propagated from seed, cultivars will not necessarily 'come **true**', so **vegetative**

methods should be used such as cuttings, layering or division to maintain stocks.

CUNEATE a term used to describe an inversely triangular or wedge-shaped leaf.

CUSHION PLANT a term applied to alpines that make bun-shaped cushions of foliage.

CUT a term used to describe leaves that are finely and deeply lobed or otherwise narrowly divided.

CUTTING a piece of stem, root or, in some cases, leaf cut from a plant and made to produce roots so that it can have an independent existence as a plant in its own right. See **greenwood cuttings, hardwood cuttings, semi-ripe cuttings, softwood cuttings**.

CUTTING-BACK (1) the process of shortening the branches of trees and shrubs.

CUTTING-BACK (2) the process of removing the dead and dying top-growth from **herbaceous perennials** in autumn.

DAMPING-DOWN the practice of watering the floor and staging of a greenhouse or conservatory in hot weather both to raise the **humidity** and to cool the house by evaporation of the water.

DAMPING-OFF a fungal disease that attacks young seedlings, rotting the stems at soil level and causing them to topple over. The risk can be minimized by sowing seeds thinly, using a well-drained compost and providing plenty of ventilation. It is to a large extent prevented if you water the compost as soon as the seeds are sown with a solution of **Cheshunt Compound**, a copper fungicide.

DEAD-HEADING the removal of spent flowers. This encourages growth by preventing seeding and also improves the appearance of many plants, particularly roses and herbaceous perennials.

DECIDUOUS a term used to describe plants that lose their leaves annually or for a season, as opposed to **evergreen** plants.

DECKCHAIR the best garden tool of all. Any gardener who leaves no time to sit and look at what he or she has created is a fool.

DECKING a style of gardening that originated in the USA and is slowly catching on in Europe. Wooden decks are laid for sitting-out areas instead of concrete or paving. When one or more edges of quite a small water feature are overlapped with decking, the effect is as if it is much larger and extends beneath the deck. Wooden decking is thought by many people to be more congenial and attractive than concrete or stone.

DECUMBENT a term used to describe a stem that lies along the ground but turns upward at the tip.

DEEP BED METHOD a **bed** system in which the beds are raised significantly by the addition of large quantities of **bulky** manure.

DEHISCENCE the splitting open of a seed pod.

DENDROLOGY the natural science of trees, as opposed to **arboriculture**, which is essentially the cultivation and care of trees.

DENTATE toothed. Often used to describe the margins of leaves.

DENTICULATE with tiny teeth.

DEPENDENT not your out-of-work aunt but a term applied to any part of a plant that hangs downward purely because of its weight. The branch of a weeping tree is not dependent. See **pendent, pendulous**.

DESICCANT a chemical used to dry plant tissues, as in drying

specimen flowers for indoor decoration.

DEWPOINT the temperature at which air becomes saturated with water vapour. As the temperature close to the ground falls to the dewpoint, dew is deposited, and if the temperature falls further to freezing, a white frost will result. It is a fallacy that the whiter the frost, the harder it is: the whiteness depends on the water content of the air.

DIBBER a tool for making holes for planting seedlings, cuttings or even for setting individual seeds. It can also be used for **pricking-out**. If you find a good one, guard it with your life. Twenty years later, I still mourn the loss of an ivory crochet hook which I used for a decade of propagating alpines commercially.

DICOTYLEDON a plant that has two seed leaves or **cotyledons**. Sometimes shortened to 'dicot'. See **monocotyledon**.

DIGITATE a term used to describe a leaf with finger-like lobes arising from a central point, as in the horse chestnut (*Aesculus hippocastanum*).

DIOECIOUS a term applied to a plant in which the male and female

flowers are borne on separate
plants. See **monoecious**.

DIPLOID a term used to describe a
plant that has two sets of **chromosomes**. Most do. The reproductive
cells have only one set.

DISBUDDING the removal of buds
to allow the unhindered
development of the remainder. It is
often employed by show growers of
exhibition chrysanthemums, for
example, as it concentrates the
energy of a plant into producing
just a few, first-class flowers. If you
want a few really fine roses, for
example, there is no reason not to
do a little disbudding here and
there. The term also applies to
the removal of shoot buds, for
example in training fruit trees
and grape vines.

DISC the central part of the
flowerhead of plants in the daisy
family, composed of tubular disc
florets and usually but not always
surrounded by a ring of more or
less flattened ray florets.

DISTRIBUTION a precise term
meaning a plant's geographical
range in nature. Thus a plant
endemic to a remote island but
grown in every temperate country,

Many fibrous-rooted herbaceous perennials
can be **DIVIDED** by placing two forks back
to back and prising them apart. Replant the
younger, outer shoots of the clump rather
than the old, central part.

does not have a wide distribution.
See also **naturalized**.

DIURNAL a term used to describe
an activity that occurs only during
the day.

DIVISION the process of propagating plants that can be split into
pieces, each of which has roots and
at least one growing point. Many
herbaceous perennials are
propagated by division.

DNA. Deoxyribonucleic acid, a
chain molecule found in
chromosomes which contains the
genetic code of an individual,
determined by the sequence of
bases arranged along its length.
The discovery of the double helix

structure of DNA opened the way for the **genetic engineering** used today to produce plants resistant to disease, for example. See **gene**.

DORMANCY when a seed cannot germinate or a plant cannot grow even though the conditions are favourable for germination or growth, it is said to be dormant. This is not the same thing as when the conditions are unfavourable, in which case the seed or plant is said to be **quiescent**. For example, corn seeds from the tombs of Pharaohs were quiescent, not dormant, but seeds of *Campanula morettiana*, which invariably pass up two perfectly suitable germination years in ideal conditions, are dormant, not quiescent.

DORSAL a term used to denote the back of a plant organ; strictly the surface that is furthest from the central axis. This is an example of the precision of botanical terms, as it includes the undersides of many leaves which you might have thought were their backs.

DOUBLE a term used to describe a flower with more than the normal number of petals and/or sepals. Sometimes a flower may be double because the reproductive organs become replaced by petals or **petaloids**, or it may be a hose-in-hose double, in which the **sepals** are the same colour and shape as the petals and give the impression of one flower inside another. See **semi-double, single**.

DOUBLE DIGGING a method of digging a plot of land to the depth of two **spits** to improve the structure of the soil and incorporate organic matter. First a trench one spit deep is dug and the soil barrowed round to the other end of the plot. Then the bottom of the trench is forked to the depth of one spit and well-rotted manure or garden compost added. When the second trench is dug, the soil is used to fill the first.

DRAINAGE (1) the way in which excess water moves in soil.

DRAINAGE (2) the means whereby excess water is removed. Some soils are naturally well drained but any that are not need artificial drainage systems, and to try to do without them is false economy. See **land drains**.

DRAW HOE a hoe whose blade is at right angles to the handle and with its edge downwards. It is very useful in the vegetable garden for earthing-up and other operations that require you to pull the surface soil towards you.

DRAWN a term used to describe plants that have become too long and thin because of poor light. It is a great mistake to overplant, as the crowding effect causes plants to become drawn. Drawn plants are weak and lose their ornamental appeal.

DRESSING a plant food given as a solid rather than a liquid – hence **top dressing**.

DRIBBLE BAR a perforated bar attached to a watering can or portable tank, used for applying weedkiller among cultivated plants. It is held close to the ground and there is no danger of spray **drift**.

DRIFT (1) drifting spray.

DRIFT (2) a large block, band or scatter of plants, e.g. a drift of daffodils, or trees planted in a drift.

DRILL a line scratched, shovelled or otherwise drawn in the soil into which seeds are sown or seedlings are planted. The name derives from the use in bygone days of a hand machine for sowing seed **broadcast** which operated by means of an oscil-

The even application of liquid lawn weedkillers can be achieved by fitting a **DRIBBLE BAR** to the watering can.

lating rod and a tightened, twisted string, in just the same way as a tool for drilling holes in wood. Drilling seed no longer means to scatter it, but to sow it in a regular manner.

DRIP LINE an imaginary line drawn beneath the extremes of the head of a tree, within which fertilizer is applied.

DRIP TIP a point at the end of a leaf from which rainwater or excessive condensation can drip. It is seen at its most effective in plants from tropical forests.

DROPPING the process of lifting a plant and then planting it again much deeper. The stems root and can be removed as new plants. It is also a method of renewing plants such as heathers if they have become lanky and over-woody. See **mound layering**.

DROUGHT a condition leading to a serious depletion of available water. It can be due to the absence of rain or to an overload of chemical salts leading to the water being locked out from the plant roots. See **osmosis**.

DUTCH HOE a hoe in which the blade is set with its cutting edge forwards. The gardener walks slowly backwards, pushing the hoe forwards. Some kinds have a push–pull action and a two-edged blade. See **draw hoe**.

DUTCH LIGHT a simple, rectangular framework, usually wooden, holding a single, large pane of glass without the use of putty or mastic. They are used either singly, as frame lights, or many at a time to make up a Dutch house, which has a pitched roof and sides that slope outwards to the ground.

DWARF an unusually small, slow-growing form of a plant. Beware of conifers that are claimed to be dwarf forms; after a few years in your garden you may find that they turn out to be slow growing but by no means small.

DWARFING the process of causing a normal sized plant to grow as if it were a dwarf. It can be done chemically, as with poinsettias (*Euphorbia pulcherrima*), by growing methods, as in **bonsai**, or by growing the plant as a **scion** on a dwarfing **rootstock**.

Comparative heights of some widely grown '**DWARF CONIFERS**' after 25 years.

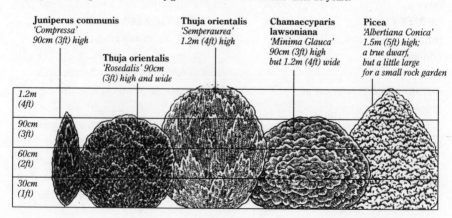

Juniperus communis
'Compressa'
90cm (3ft) high

Thuja orientalis
'Rosedalis' 90cm
(3ft) high and wide

Thuja orientalis
'Semperaurea'
1.2m (4ft) high

Chamaecyparis
lawsoniana
'Minima Glauca'
90cm (3ft) high
but 1.2m (4ft) wide

Picea
'Albertiana Conica'
1.5m (5ft) high;
a true dwarf,
but a little large
for a small rock garden

1.2m (4ft)
90cm (3ft)
60cm (2ft)
30cm (1ft)

EARTHING-UP the practice of drawing soil up around a plant or its lower parts, usually done with a **draw hoe** and used in cultivating potatoes and in **blanching** leeks and celery.

ECOLOGY the study of the relationships between organisms and between them and the environment. Ecology is a branch of biological science – it is not enough merely to have an interest in natural history or to feel strongly about man's influence on his surroundings to consider yourself an ecologist.

ECOSYSTEM a community of organisms and its environment. A termites' nest is an ecosystem, as is the planet as a whole.

EDGING (1) the process of making neat edges to a lawn either using edging irons, or by laying plastic or metal strips.

EDGING (2) plants grown alongside a path or the verge of a flower bed or a plantation of shrubs. A popular form of edging is alternate plants of white alyssum and blue lobelia – the gardening equivalent of flying ducks on the wall of the lounge.

EDGING IRON a medium-handled tool with a half-moon blade, often most reasonably called a half-moon.

EELWORMS (NEMATODES) a huge family of worm-like animals, most of which are too small to be seen with the naked eye. They are major pests of agriculture and horticulture worldwide, although are less common in colder countries. Eelworms can affect potatoes and tomatoes (cyst eelworms), chrysanthemums, begonias and strawberries (leaf and bud eelworms), and phloxes, daffodils and onions (stem and bulb eelworms). Control is not easy and **rotation** of crops and the 'clean' propagation of some plants (for example by **micropropagation**) are the best preventative measures.

ELECTRONIC LEAF seldom electronic but always electrical, this is a moisture detector in a greenhouse to tell a **mist propagation** unit when to switch on the water.

ELM BARK BEETLE see **bark beetles.**

EMBRYO the potential plant within the seed.

ENDEMIC *(NOUN AND ADJECTIVE)* a plant that occurs naturally in one place only. A plant may be endemic to a particular tract of land, a geographical area (such as the Dolomites), a country, or a continent (e.g. the genus Eucalyptus is endemic to Australia and Tasmania).

ENTIRE a term used to describe leaf margins that have no lobes or teeth.

ENZYME a protein that assists in a chemical action within an organism without being changed itself.

EPIPHYTE a plant that grows on another plant but is not parasitic. Many tropical orchids, for example, are epiphytic, but mistletoes are not.

ERICACEOUS (1) a plant belonging to the family Ericaceae, which includes heathers and rhododendrons among many others.

ERICACEOUS (2) a term used to describe lime-free composts formulated for use with ericaceous plants, which are mostly lime-haters or **calcifuges.**

ESCAPE a garden plant that becomes **naturalized** in the surrounding area.

ESPALIER a way of supporting and training fruit trees so that they grow horizontally along wires from short uprights.

ETHNOBOTANY the study of humankind's relationships with plants, which essentially has to do with their roles as medicines and foods. As studies are made of the remains of the rain forests, and as the importance of the plants to humankind becomes more and more apparent, this presently somewhat obscure term will become much better known.

ETHYLENE a gas given off by ripe fruit that acts as a hormone, promoting the ripening of fruit. It is also produced by damaged or grazed trees and shrubs and acts as a communicating agent between them. Undamaged trees downwind will be encouraged to produce bitter-tasting tannins. This is why giraffes, which browse on acacias, usually work their way upwind from tree to tree.

ETIOLATED the same as **drawn**.

EVAPORATION the process by which a liquid turns into a gas. In the garden it usually refers to the conversion of water to water vapour.

EVAPOTRANSPIRATION the loss of water from a plant via a combination of **evaporation** and **transpiration**.

EVERGREEN this does not mean that the leaves stay on for ever but that some of the foliage remains green for at least one year, as opposed to **deciduous** plants which lose their leaves for a season. Few leaves last longer than three years. Although it implies that the leaves are green, it is also of course applied to plants that have gold, yellow, red or variegated foliage as well. See **deciduous**.

EVERLASTING a term applied to certain flowers, usually of a papery consistency, that last a long time when dried.

EXFOLIATING a term used to describe bark that peels in papery layers.

EXOTIC originally, this was a term that meant no more than 'foreign' – a plant introduced from another country. Thus, for example, the Oxford ragwort (*Senecio squalidus*) that spread along the railway lines after being introduced to Britain is, correctly, an exotic, even though it is entirely lacking in glamour. Today, however, exotic is so often used to mean 'attractively unusual or bizarre, tropical-looking', that this must be taken as perfectly proper usage.

EYE (1) a latent bud, such as those on a potato.

EYE (2) the centre of a flower if of a contrasting colour or if it shows different structures, as in primulas (**pin-eyed** and **thrum-eyed**).

EYE (3) a piece of stem with just one lateral bud, such as is taken for propagating grape vines.

F₁ HYBRIDS the term 'F₁' stands for first filial generation and indicates the first generation offspring of a cross between two pure-bred plants. F₁ hybrids are usually particularly strong, high yielding (in the case of vegetables) and, in ornamental plants, free flowering with uniform or predictably mixed colours. Uniformity is a prime quality of F₁ hybrids. They are costly to produce and you must expect to pay more for F₁ seed or plants. See **hybrid**.

F₂ HYBRIDS second filial generation hybrids, produced by crossing **F₁ hybrids**, are not as uniform as the first filial generation but are generally desirable plants and the seed or seedlings will be less expensive. See **hybrid**.

FALCATE a term used to describe leaves that are sickle-shaped.

FALL (1) one of the outer **perianth** segments of an iris flower, usually drooping or horizontal (flared).

FALL (2) autumn in America (where it is also called autumn). Increasingly used in the UK and Ireland but as yet mainly with reference to the turning of the leaves.

FAMILY a term often misunderstood by gardeners. It is a category of plants larger than **genus** and contains a number of related genera. For example, the family Ericaceae includes the genera *Erica, Cassiope, Andromeda* and *Rhododendron*. There is therefore no such thing as the 'erica family' or the 'rhododendron family'. On the other hand, you can speak of the Ericaceae as the 'heather family', just as the the lily family, Liliaceae, includes *Agave*, *Allium* and *Agapanthus* and many more besides *Lilium* itself.

FAMILY TREE not a table of descent but a tree bearing two or more distinct kinds of fruit that have been grafted on to a common **rootstock**.

FAN-TRAINED a term used to describe a fruit tree that has been trained so that its branches arise from a central point on a short stem and radiate out like a fan. Used for peaches and nectarines but also attractive on a north-facing wall, where a fan-trained Morello cherry will succeed.

FANCY a term used by fanciers to denote variegated flowers.

FARINA a powdery or mealy coating on leaves, stems and flowers, especially primulas: a form of **bloom**. The adjective is farinaceous.

FASCIATION a condition in which plant parts fuse. You may see, for instance, a primula with several stems fused sideways-on to look like a liquorice strap, or the 'cockscomb' type of celosia flower, which is several fused together.

FASTIGIATE a term used to describe trees and shrubs that have an erect **habit** with a narrow **crown** and almost vertical branches.

FEATHERED a term used to describe a young tree with a slender main stem and several lateral, feathery branches.

FERNERY essentially a concept popular in Victorian times, when ferns were grown in grottoes, dells, greenhouses, or even glass cases.

FERRUGINEOUS rust-coloured.

FERTILIZATION in gardening, a term loosely used to refer to the deposition of pollen on the **pistil**. More correctly, it is the union of the male and female cells.

FERTILIZER a material that provides plant nutrients in a relatively concentrated form. It may be **inorganic** or **organic**, synthetic or natural, liquid, powder or granular. A compound fertilizer contains more than one nutrient – often the three major **macronutrients**, nitrogen, phosphorus and potassium (**NPK**).

FIBROUS ROOTS root systems consisting of a mass of fine roots as opposed to those with much fewer, coarser, more woody ones. Plants with fibrous roots are more easily moved than those with long, thick ones. See **tap root**.

FIELD CAPACITY ground is said to be at field capacity when it is holding all the water it can against the force of gravity, i.e. when the drains stop running.

FILAMENT (I) a thread-like organ, hair or appendage, such as the filaments on the edges of the leaves of some yuccas.

FILAMENT (2) the stalk of an **anther**. Filament and anther together make up a **stamen**.

FIMBRIATE a term used to describe a leaf or petal with a frilly fringe.

FISH MANURE powdered fish waste; a fertilizer relatively high in phosphorus. The destruction of fish stocks for the fertilizer market is an environmental problem that receives little attention.

FLAG a flat stone usually used for paving.

FLAMED a term used to describe flowers (particularly tulips) with feathered petals, each of which has a central band of colour.

FLOCCULATION when lime is added to a clay soil, the particles can form larger crumbs and the soil is said to have been flocculated. It becomes easier to work and better drained.

FLORA (I) the entire wild plant population of a continent, country or part of a country.

FLORA (2) a book describing the flora of an area, as in *Flora Europaea* or *The Flora of The Lesser Antilles*.

FLORE PLENO literally, 'with double flowers', it is often used as a name for garden varieties with **double** flowers.

FLORET a very small flower, usually one of several or many gathered into an inflorescence, as in a daisy or a hydrangea. See **ray floret**.

FLORIFEROUS a term used to describe a plant that bears its flowers generously. A free-flowering plant.

FLORIST'S (I) a term applied to flowers grown not, primarily, for sale in flower shops, but for exhibition.

FLORIST'S (2) a term applied to names used in the flower trade that are incorrect or out of date. For example, the florist's mimosa is *Acacia dealbata* and not a mimosa at all, and the arum lily is neither an arum nor a lily but *Zantedeschia aethiopica*.

FLOWER a flower can consist of as little as one **stamen** or one **pistil**, or both. If a flower has a **perianth** (sepals and petals) it is termed perfect. Flowers can be male or female or both. Flowers exist to assist pollination by attracting pollinators such as bees, birds, moths and butterflies.

FLOWER GATHERER secateurs made to hold the cut stem.

FLUID SOWING the process of sowing in a fluid gel seeds that have been pre-germinated. See **chitting**.

FLUSH a burst of flowering or fruiting. 'The first flush of roses' or 'a flush of fungi'.

FOG apart from the usual meaning, fog is the next stage in sophistication after **mist propagation**. The water is converted to fog particles and controlled by computer. Its advantage is that the undersides as well as the upper surfaces of the leaves of the cuttings become coated with moisture. Its main disadvantages are expense, which effectively restricts its use to large, professional set-ups, and the clogging of the fog nozzles by lime deposits.

FOLIAGE PLANT (1) in the UK and Ireland, a plant grown principally for the attractiveness of its foliage.

FOLIAGE PLANT (2) in the USA, a house plant.

FOLIAR FEEDING applying fertilizer to plants in the form of a liquid that is watered on to the leaves. It should be neither long-term nor routine, but primarily used to correct a fault. Not to be confused with **liquid feeding**.

FOLLY a building or structure put up with no purpose other than to be a focal point or simply for fun.

FORCING the process of producing early flowering or fruiting by changing the growing conditions. The most common example of forcing is the starting of hyacinths in fibre in heat and darkness to gain very early flowers. Exhibitors at the Chelsea Flower Show in London,

FORCING rhubarb by excluding all light produces an early crop of very tender sticks.

(a) Dig up the crown and cut into three or four sections, each with a growing point.

(b) Place the crowns in boxes of compost or good garden soil and put them under the greenhouse staging.

(c) Surround the box with sacking or black material to exclude light from the developing stems.

A forcing pot lightly filled with straw can be placed over rhubarb crowns outside: the lid can be removed to check how sticks are developing. They will not be as early as those forced in a warm greenhouse.

FORMAL GARDEN a garden made up of geometrical forms, straight lines and angles, with patterns playing a large part and usually featuring fountains, statues and clipped hedges as well as flowers.

FORMATIVE PRUNING the early pruning, especially of fruit trees, that establishes the final form.

FRAME see **cold frame**.

FRAMEWORK (1) the branch structure of a tree or shrub.

FRAMEWORK (2) in garden design, the structure of a planting scheme, provided mainly by evergreen trees and shrubs.

FRENCH LAYERING also known as continuous or ground layering, this is a way of propagating plants that have long, flexible shoots near the ground. The shoots are pegged down or buried at intervals and form roots at these points. The links between them can be cut when rooting is well established to give a series of new plants.

which is held at the end of May, force roses and other flowers to the limits of perfection. The opposite of **retarding**.

FOREST BARK see **bark (shredded)**.

FOREST TRANSPLANT a very young, very small tree seedling, ideal for planting in difficult places. It is a legitimate term that is in danger of being used as a marketing ploy for 'we forgot this one'.

FRIABLE a term used to describe a soil that is crumbly and easily worked. Stiff clay is not friable, but then neither is pure sand.

FRIT (FRITS) a fine powder made by fusing **trace elements** into glass, which is then ground up. It is applied particularly to potting compost or used as a **top dressing**. The process ensures slow release of the trace elements.

FROND the leaf of a fern or palm. It is not incorrect, however, to refer to a 'fern leaf' or to say that a palm has leaves.

FROST DAMAGE this is essentially caused in plants by the expansion of water as it freezes in the cells. It is prevented or lessened when starches are changed into sugars, which happens in late summer and autumn in the wood-ripening process, as the freezing point of sugars is lower than that of water. Plants also express water from their cells into the spaces between them, where expansion does no damage. Frost damage shows up as die-back of branchlets, the death of buds, blackening or other marking of leaves and bark-split.

FROST HEAVE when water in the soil turns to ice, it expands and tends to thrust newly planted plants out of the ground. You should always check recent plantings after hard frost and firm down gently any that have risen.

FROST POCKET see **air drainage**.

FRUIT the fertilized ovary of a flower after it has ripened, along with any other flower parts that assist in the formation of the fruit. It is by no means necessarily a juicy thing to eat.

FUNGUS belonging neither to the Plant Kingdom nor the Animal Kingdom, the fungi include the mushrooms, moulds, rusts and yeasts and are simple organisms lacking chlorophyll. Many are important agents of plant disease in the garden, for example **honey fungus** and powdery **mildew**.

FYM a somewhat coy abbreviation for farmyard manure.

GALL a swelling, usually caused by an insect.

GARDEN a piece of ground on which an eclectic mixture of plants is grown – as opposed to a field, in which there is little variety and the plants are grown exclusively as crops or fodder. Horticulture is the cultivation of gardens; agriculture that of fields.

GARDEN LINE not a steam railway for tourists but a string with a stick at either end, used for guidance when making straight lines or circles.

GARDENESQUE a term you will come across in books on garden history. It was a nineteenth-century idea that suggested making a garden more like art than nature.

GARDENING of all human activities the one that attracts the greatest extremes of love and hate – occasionally within the same individual.

GAZEBO much the same as a **belvedere**.

GENE part of a **chromosome** carrying the code for the heredity of a particular set of characters in an individual.

GENETIC ENGINEERING a recently developed technique in which genes for a desirable characteristic, such as resistance to a particular disease, are transferred from one plant to another. It is likely to have considerable impact on both gardening and agriculture in the not too distant future.

GENETICS the study of heredity.

GENUS the rank between **family** and **species**. It consists of either a number of species that share common, distinctive characteristics or, occasionally, just one species that is highly distinctive, in which case the genus is said to be **monotypic**. The name of the genus is the first element in the Latin name of a plant. Thus in *Calluna vulgaris* the genus is *Calluna*. See **binomial system, naming of plants**.

GEOTROPISM the movement or growth of a plant or part of a plant in response to gravity. Roots are usually positively geotropic and grow downwards; most stems are negatively geotropic.

GERMINATION the process of a seed's 'waking up' and beginning to grow, usually considered complete with the appearance of the seed leaves or **cotyledons**.

GIRDLING the removal of a ring of bark from the trunk of a tree, also known as ring-barking. It prevents plant food reaching the roots and causes the death of the tree. The damage can be caused by deer, rabbits or squirrels or by

mechanical damage such as the rubbing of a loose tree tie.

GLABROUS a term used to describe a smooth and hairless stem, leaf or other plant part.

GLANDULAR plants, as well as animals, have glands, but they are on the surfaces of leaves and stems or sometimes in the tips of hairs. They may secrete poisons to deter predators, as in stinging nettles (*Urtica*), or resins, oils or nectar. See **nectary**.

GLASSHOUSE the same as **greenhouse**.

GLAUCOUS a term applied to any part of a plant covered with a white, grey or bluish **bloom**.

GLOBOSE a term used to describe any part of a plant, such as a fruit, or even a whole plant that is almost but not quite spherical.

GLOBULAR in ordinary English this means spherical, but in botany it has the special meaning of being made up of things that are globose. A blackberry is globular.

GRAFT UNION the point on the stem of a plant where the **scion**

and **rootstock** were united. It is usually visible as a slight swelling and it is as well to examine it closely when buying a plant that has been grafted. If it looks weak, cracked or not properly sealed, or if it looks as if it is only very recently established, you should reject the plant. There is no greater disappointment than spending good money on a grafted tree, planting it with happy anticipation, only to find the graft union has come apart or become a site for disease. You can seldom take it back and ask for a refund, so it is better to be careful. Never bury the graft union when planting unless given specific instructions to do so (as with tree peonies).

GRAFTING (1) a method of propagation in which a **scion** is joined to a **rootstock** so that they fuse and make one plant.

GRAFTING (2) digging drainage ditches, often with a special spade known as a grafting tool.

GRAFTING (3) getting down to the hard work. The term is derived from (2) above.

GRAPE SCISSORS scissors with very slender, long blades, used for thinning bunches of grapes.

GRASSING-DOWN the practice of sowing grass around fruit trees in order to slow down the growth and encourage more fruits. It is becoming less desirable as fruit **rootstocks** improve and is not recommended for ornamental trees.

GREASE-BAND a ring of sticky or greasy material attached round the trunk of a tree to prevent wingless insects from climbing it. It is used particularly in fruit growing to deter wingless female moths but also in ornamental gardening against such creatures as vine weevils, which can disfigure the leaves of trees.

GREEN MANURE this is a fast-growing crop grown in a bed that is empty for a period of time and then dug in to provide organic matter and plant food. Members of the pea family are especially valuable as green manure because they can fix nitrogen from the atmosphere and add it to the soil.

GREENHOUSE a glass structure, defined by its being large enough for a gardener to enter and stand up in it and expressly used for the cultivation of plants. (A dwelling house constructed of glass bricks –

and there are such things – is not a greenhouse and neither are any of the glass skyscrapers in Dallas.)

GREENSAND strictly speaking this is a sandstone, but as far as gardeners are concerned it is the type of soil derived from it and is among the very best for growing the widest possible range of plants.

GREENWOOD CUTTINGS these cuttings are between 'soft' and 'semi-ripe'.

GREX a collective word, literally meaning 'flock', originally applied to all the **cultivars** from the same cross. Its use is reserved these days for orchids, which is just as well, because although its purpose and rationale are no doubt eminently clear to botanists, the concept is confusing in the extreme to gardeners.

GREY MOULD see **botrytis**.

GRIT fairly obvious, you might think, but specifically sharp-edged material between large-grained sand and small pea-gravel. It is a first-class material for drainage in composts and is used extensively for alpine plants for that purpose and as a protective **top dressing**. Grits may be derived from

various kinds of rocks but are similar in physical characteristics.

GROTTO an artificial cave or stone bower, usually somewhat whimsical. Grottoes have been garden features for 2000 years but were never so popular or peculiar as in Victorian times. The word has the same root as 'grotesque', which is not at all surprising. Nowadays the chief inhabitants of garden grottoes are plastic gnomes. Why not? They might as well be.

GROUND FROST this occurs when the air temperature at the soil surface or just a little above it drops to freezing or below. It happens when heat is lost to the atmosphere through radiation and is common on clear nights. Ground frost is rarely damaging to plants unless accompanied by **air frost** and many tender plants such as oleanders, bottle-brushes and several palms can go through quite a few ground frosts in a season without any harm coming to them.

GROUND LAYERING see **French layering**.

GROUNDCOVER spreading, ground-hugging plants that will grow with little attention and cover the ground so that weeds are suppressed and maintenance is greatly reduced. There is something of a cult of groundcover, which is not necessarily a good thing.

GROWING BAG, GROW BAG a plastic bale containing soil-less compost, in which plants, especially tomatoes and courgettes, are grown directly. They are sometimes also used for orna-mentals on terraces, balconies and paved areas.

GROWING-ON the process of actively encouraging the development of plants beyond the propagation stage.

GROWING POINT the growing tip of a stem.

GROWMORE a balanced fertilizer developed during the Second World War by the British Ministry of Agriculture containing 7 per cent nitrogen, 7 per cent phosphorus and 7 per cent potassium. It is excellent.

GROWTH REGULATORS chemi-cals used primarily by commercial growers to change the rates at which plants grow. They are used, for example, to produce compact pot plants such as poinsettias and chrysanthemums.

GUM a sticky substance found in many trees and shrubs. It is sometimes exuded from the bark, especially of pines and some species of *Prunus*, as a result of disease, when it is known as 'gumming'.

GUYING the practice of supporting a tree by means of (usually) three cables attached to a common point on the tree and to pegs driven into the ground at equal distances from one another. It is used for trees that are too large to be staked.

GYMNOSPERM a member of a group of plants whose seeds are exposed, rather than enclosed in an ovary. Conifers and the primitive cycads are gymnosperms. See **angiosperm**.

HA-HA a ditch, gradually sloping on one side and almost vertical on the other, usually with the steep side retained by a wall, designed to keep cattle out of a garden without there being a visible boundary between it and the fields. They are found mainly on large country properties and mainly date from the eighteenth and nineteenth centuries, but are occasionally still constructed.

HABIT the general way in which a plant grows. Plants have, among others, weeping, erect, columnar, spreading or compact habits.

HABITAT the sort of place in which a plant is found in the wild. It refers to the climate, aspect, altitude, soil and interaction with other organisms. The term is not generally used in relation to cultivation, although you can create a habitat in the garden for a plant – or animal for that matter.

HALF-HARDY a term applied to annual or perennial plants that cannot stand frost and are therefore grown as annuals in frost-prone areas. They are either sown in warmth and planted out when all danger of frost has passed, or they are sown in situ when the weather is warm enough.

HALF-MOON see **edging iron**.

HALF-POT a short plant pot, used for plants with shallow roots or those, such as some alpines or cacti, that demand fierce drainage.

HALF-RIPE see **semi-ripe**.

HAND FORK a small tool, usually four-tined, for lifting small plants and

Rooting **HARDWOOD** cuttings outdoors.

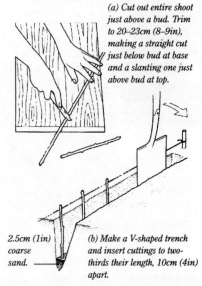

(a) Cut out entire shoot just above a bud. Trim to 20–23cm (8–9in), making a straight cut just below bud at base and a slanting one just above bud at top.

2.5cm (1in) coarse sand.

(b) Make a V-shaped trench and insert cuttings to two-thirds their length, 10cm (4in) apart.

weeding. Its weak point is where it meets the handle, and a cheap hand fork is a bad investment, as it will buckle in heavy soil.

HARDENING-OFF the process of acclimatizing plants to conditions that require greater **hardiness** than the ones they have just left. Seedlings grown in the greenhouse should never be planted straight out into the garden without hardening-off. First, ventilation should be increased for a few days, then the plants should be moved to a cold frame or taken outdoors during the day. Finally, the plants should be left outdoors unprotected for about a week before being planted out.

HARDINESS a relative term that often causes confusion amongst gardeners. A plant is said to be hardy if it will survive all year round in the climatic conditions that prevail where it is grown. Thus a plant hardy in the south of Britain will not necessarily be so in the north and one that is hardy in both areas would be said to be fully hardy in the context of the British Isles but it might not thrive in Moscow. Hardiness depends on such things as soil, drainage, amount of sun and warmth received, shelter from winds, nutrition, age and general health, all of which vary from garden to garden, and it is thus impossible to make dogmatic statements about the hardiness of any plant. The USA is divided into ten climatic zones used to specify hardiness. See **half-hardy, tender**.

HARDPAN a layer in the soil that prevents the movement of water. Hardpan can be caused by leaching of soil minerals, which gather at a certain depth and form an impermeable layer, or it can be caused by the use of machines such as rotavators, in which case it will be closer to the surface. Hardpan is quite common in sandy soils and renders them boggy, when they might be expected to be dry.

HARDWOOD the timber obtained from broad-leaf trees.

HARDWOOD CUTTINGS these cuttings are taken late in the season and consist of fully matured wood. Usually from **deciduous** trees and shrubs after the leaves have fallen, they are usually rooted in a trench in the open garden.

HAULMS the stalks of certain plants, including potatoes, peas and beans and cereal crops.

HEADING-BACK the process of reducing the head of a tree or shrub by shortening all its main branches, usually quite severely.

HEARTWOOD the inner layers of the stem of a woody plant. The function of heartwood is to provide strength, while the transport of water and nutrients goes on in the outer sapwood. It is usually darker in colour than sapwood (in ebony, for instance, it is black, while the sapwood is dark brown). Once the heartwood of a tree has become infected with fungi, it is inevitable that it will have to be felled, otherwise it will one day crash without warning. Tree preservation orders, which affect many gardeners, should allow for such felling, but proper evidence must be brought forward.

HEATH a term used to distinguish Erica species from *Calluna vulgaris*, which some admit as the only heather. It is a matter of opinion, but as the distinction is not made in ordinary speech, perhaps it could be dispensed with in gardening.

HEATHER GARDEN a garden or part of a garden in which heaths and heathers are grown together, often interspersed with dwarf and slow-growing conifers and other appropriate shrubs.

HEEL a strip of bark taken from the old wood when a **cutting** is removed from a tree or shrub.

HEELING-IN putting plants (usually **bare-rooted** plants) temporarily in the soil while waiting – for weather or convenience – to plant them.

HELIOTROPIC a term applied to a plant or part of a plant that turns to follow the sun. Seedlings on a windowsill exhibit this behaviour as they bend towards the light.

HERB (1) in ordinary use in Britain, a culinary or medicinal plant.

HERB (2) in botany, any herbaceous plant.

HERB (3) in the USA, a herbaceous plant or a culinary or medicinal plant. Always pronounced *'erb*.

HERBACEOUS BORDER a border devoted to **herbaceous perennials**. See **mixed border**.

HERBACEOUS PERENNIAL strictly speaking, any non-woody **perennial** plant, including such things as bergenias and phormiums, but in gardening terms it means a plant that dies down for the winter.

HERBAL the name given in the seventeenth century to any book on plants but now restricted to those of culinary or medicinal use.

HERBARIUM a systematic collection of preserved plant specimens. It also refers to the room or building in which the collection is housed.

HERBICIDE a chemical for destroying weeds.

HONEY FUNGUS a major disease of trees and shrubs and one with which we must unfortunately learn to live with for there is no cure. It spreads via the roots of plants and produces black bootlace-like rhizomorphs, creamy white mycelia and orange 'toadstools'. Many different ornamental and fruit trees and shrubs are susceptible. It is important to remove old tree stumps to reduce the chances of honey fungus gaining a hold in your garden.

HONEYDEW a sticky liquid produced by sap-sucking insects, notably **aphids**. Insects feeding on a tree cause a sticky deposit on anything below, including your newly polished car (under a lime tree). If the deposit is allowed to accumulate on the foliage of shrubs such as camellias, black moulds can quickly grow and suffocate the leaves. This

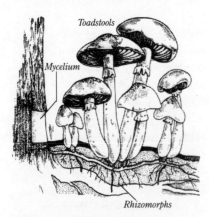

Toadstools

Mycelium

Rhizomorphs

HONEY FUNGUS rhizomorphs travel through the soil, penetrate the bark and form a compact, creamy-white fungal sheet (mycelium) under the bark. Toadstools may be formed in the autumn.

is best prevented by getting rid of the aphids as soon as they are seen.

HOOF AND HORN a slow-release fertilizer with a high proportion of nitrogen, useful for giving a boost to overwintered plants, such as cabbages, in the spring.

HORMONE a complex natural chemical produced in one part of a plant but with its action in another. Hormones control plant growth and do so at very low concentrations. If you use artificial hormones such as rooting powders you should do so sparingly. See **auxins**.

HORTICULTURE the art of cultivating gardens. It is increasingly a science as well but, like medicine, will always remain an art. Flair, talent, inspiration and aesthetics will always dominate on the ornamental side, while such objective matters as acceptable texture and flavour count for much in the kitchen garden.

HOSE-IN-HOSE see **double**.

HOST PLANT strictly, any plant that has a parasite growing on or in it, as an apple tree with mistletoe. Gardeners use the term sometimes when discussing growing one plant over another but not parasitically, as when a tree is the host plant to a clematis.

HOT BED not what you might think, but a **cold frame** at the bottom of which is deep layer of decomposing manure. This gives off heat as it ferments and keeps the plants in the frame warm. Horse manure is the best kind. Hot beds are said to have become out of date but many a country gardener and quite a few in towns use them rather than incur the expense of installing and running heating cables. Hot-bed handles are brass or gunmetal handles screwed to the frame light for ease of handling.

HOT HOUSE see **stove house**.

HOUSE PLANT a tough but non-hardy plant that grows well in a dwelling house. They are more often grown for their foliage than their flowers and in the USA are collectively known as 'foliage' or 'foliage plants'.

HUMIDITY the amount of water vapour in the air. It should not be confused with steam, which is a visible suspension of liquid droplets. It is important to maintain humidity levels in the greenhouse in the summer by **damping-down**

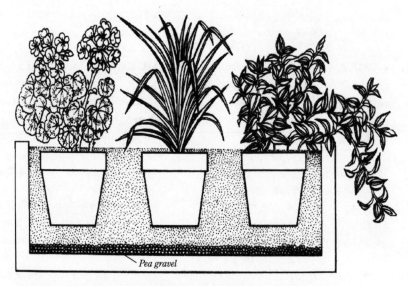

It is important to maintain the **HUMIDITY** around house plants. This can be achieved by grouping them in a container filled with moist peat.

the floor periodically. Lack of humidity often causes problems for house plants in centrally heated houses, leading to leaf scorching and attack by red spider **mites**. It can be counteracted by grouping plants together, by spraying the leaves with water or by standing pots in a larger container of moist peat or gravel.

HUMUS there is almost universal misunderstanding among gardeners of the nature of humus. It is *not* a fibrous substance. Leaf mould, horse manure, farmyard manure, peat and so on are not humus, but humus precursors – they break down to form humus. Humus is an amorphous, black or dark brown gel, much more like cold gravy than anything fibrous. It gives the soil its dark colour, enabling it to hold more heat; it provides a source of slowly released nitrogen and phosphorus; it plays a vital part in soil structure, especially in clays; and it helps sandy soils to retain water.

HYBRID the offspring of plants belonging to two different taxa (plant categories). Hybrids may be either natural or, more commonly, manmade and they may be between two species of the same genus (interspecific hybrids) or between two species of different genera (intergeneric). For example, x *Cupressocyparis leylandii*, the ever-present Leyland cypress, is an intergeneric hybrid between *Cupressus macrocarpa* and *Chamaecyparis nootkatensis*.

HYBRID VIGOUR some hybrids, especially first-generation ones (F_1 **hybrids**), show strength, freedom of flowering, greater yield or resistance to disease than either parent.

HYDROPONICS a method of horticulture in which no soil is used, nutrients being delivered to the plants in a solution in water.

IMBRICATE a term used to describe plant parts, usually leaves, that are overlapping like roof tiles.

IMMORTELLE another word for an **everlasting**.

IMPRESSED a term used to describe leaf veins that are sunk into the surface.

INCOMPATIBLE (1) when one plant cannot fertilize another the two are said to be incompatible. When buying fruit trees you should always make sure that the varieties are compatible, otherwise you may have no fruit.

INCOMPATIBLE (2) if a **rootstock** will not make a permanent, stable union with a **scion** in grafting, the two are said to be incompatible.

INDUMENTUM a covering of hairs. An indumentum may be woolly, flocculose (much the same as woolly but less so) or plastered (smooth and glossy). Sometimes an indumentum will be referred to as 'felt' or 'felted'.

INFLATED a term used to describe a plant part that appears blown up, although of course it has not been. The lips of calceoarias and some orchids are said to be inflated.

INFLORESCENCE the arrangement of flowers on a stem. There are many different types of inflorescence from the long dangling **racemes** of wisteria to the dense, rounded heads of the drumstick primula (*Primula denticulata*). Sometimes, what we loosely refer to as a 'flower' is, in fact, an inflorescence. For example, the flowerhead of a hydrangea is an inflorescence made up of several small flowers or **florets**.

INFORMAL a term applied to gardens that are not laid out in geometrical shapes but are more loose in structure, such as rock gardens or woodland gardens. Most home gardens tend to be a mixture of formal and informal features, which is no bad thing.

INORGANIC FERTILIZER of neither animal nor vegetable origin, inorganic fertilizers provide plant nutrients in concentrated form but do not improve soil texture. However, this is no reason to dispense with them altogether and they can be very effective provided they are used at the recommended rates and that attention is also paid to conditioning the soil. Inorganic fertilizers are not necessarily synthetic and many are made from naturally occurring minerals. See **organic fertilizer**.

INSECTICIDE a substance used to kill insects. See **contact insecticide**, **systemic**.

INSECTIVOROUS PLANTS these are plants that have evolved to be able to survive in low-nitrogen environments, such as bogs, making up the deficiency by trapping insects and reducing them to a solution of proteins that they can absorb.

INTERCROPPING the practice of growing a rapidly maturing crop between the rows of a slower one. It is often confused with **catch cropping**.

INTERNODE the part of a stem between two **nodes**.

INTERSPECIFIC CROSS a cross between two species. See **hybrid**.

INTRASPECIFIC a cross within a species. See **hybrid**.

INVOLUCRE one or more conspicuous **bracts** around an **inflorescence**. The flowerheads of *Cornus kousa* are surrounded by an involucre of creamy white bracts.

IRISHMAN'S CUTTING a scandalous expression denoting a piece of a plant (usually a shrub or climber), already provided with roots, which can be separated as an independent plant. It is profoundly to be hoped that such calumny will be found to have no place among the better types of gardeners.

ISLAND BED a bed of hardy perennials, usually surrounded by lawn. It is a term that is quite astonishingly recent, given the eminently sensible nature of the concept it describes. Alan Bloom, nurseryman of Norfolk, pioneered the use of island beds in his garden, where customers could walk right round them and see the plants featured in the nursery list. Horticulturally it is an excellent idea, with the plants receiving maximum light and air. From a design point of view it can hardly be bettered for making the maximum use of a relatively small garden.

JAPANESE GARDENS attempts to make Japanese gardens outside Japan run the danger of looking and being ridiculous. Only a very few amateur gardeners have succeeded and many professionals have failed. The faults tend to be tweeness and a tendency towards garden gnomism, combined with a lack of understanding of what Japanese gardening styles (of which there are many) are all about. See **Zen garden**.

JARDINIÈRE an ornamental container in which house plants are stood complete with their pots. It can also be a stand for them. These days it is often called a 'planter'.

JOHN INNES COMPOSTS these are soil-based composts developed (but not manufactured) at the John Innes Horticultural Institute in Norwich. They are made to a formula that defines the proportions of loam, peat and sand and they contain the John Innes base fertilizer, which consists of two parts nitrogen as **hoof and horn**, two parts **superphosphate** and one part **potassium sulphate**.

JOINT the point where a leaf is attached to a stem. A botanist would more accurately use the term 'node', as in 'take the cutting at a node', which means just below a leaf joint.

JUNE DROP the natural dropping of immature fruit from **top fruits**, especially apples, at around midsummer. It varies in quantity from year to year and is perfectly normal.

JUVENILE FOLIAGE see **adult foliage**.

KATABATICS the study of the flow of wind under the influence of temperature. It is important in understanding **air frost** and **frost pockets** and how to avoid trapping plants in places where the effects of frost are made even more severe. The downward flow of cold air in the garden is a miniature version of the katabatic winds that occur when cold air sinks swiftly down from snowy mountain tops in summer.

KEEL the boat-shaped, lower fused petals of a pea-type flower.

KEY (1) the winged seed of a plant such as maple or ash.

KEY (2) a system of identifying a plant by yes/no pairs of propositions.

KNOT GARDEN a formal bed arranged in a complicated pattern, often maze-like, with miniature hedges of clipped box (*Buxus sempervirens*), lavender (*Lavendula*), cotton lavender (*Santolina*) or similar plants. Knot gardens were very fashionable in the sixteenth century and are enjoying something of a revival. The 'background' is sometimes filled with low-growing annuals or other seasonal plants or is left with a gravel or sand base. As with **Japanese gardens**, knot gardens *can* look wonderful but can also appear highly pretentious.

LACED a term applied to garden pinks with scalloped edges to the petals, picked out in a contrasting colour. *Dianthus* 'Dad's Favourite' is a laced old-fashioned pink and *D.* 'London Poppet' is a modern one.

LADYBIRDS several species of beetles with coloured wing cases, usually red but sometimes yellow or even black, that bear anything from two to twenty-two spots. They are beneficial insects that, in both adult and larval forms, feed on aphids, scale insects and mites.

LANCEOLATE a term applied to leaves or bracts that are shaped like a lance.

LAND DRAINS pipes laid in the soil to carry away excess water. They used to be made of earthenware but are now almost exclusively plastic.

LANDSCAPE GARDENING originally a style of gardening made popular in the eighteenth century by the Englishman Capability Brown. It involved changing the surroundings of a large country house so that it blended with the countryside as a whole and was a reaction against the excessive formalism of the time.

LARVA the immature form, usually completely different in appearance from the adult, into which insects hatch from the egg. Larvae are often wingless but highly mobile caterpillers, grubs or maggots with voracious appetites. Some, such as ladybird larvae, are beneficial in the garden; many are serious pests.

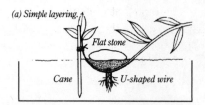

(a) Simple layering.

Flat stone

Cane   U-shaped wire

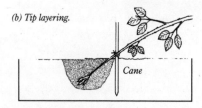

(b) Tip layering.

Cane

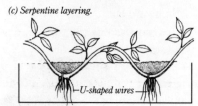

(c) Serpentine layering.

—U-shaped wires—

(d) Continuous layering.

Mounding to encourage root growth

U-shaped wire

LAYERING.

LATENT BUDS buds that do not grow until something, such as the removal of the tip bud, encourages them to do so. Dormant buds are the same thing, but some teachers and writers distinguish between the two according to whether they

are visible or hidden beneath the bark. See **eye** (1).

LATEX a milky, slightly sticky sap produced by a number of plants, such as dandelions, euphorbias and lettuce. Its purpose is not fully understood, but it is quite often irritating to the skin, if not poisonous.

LATH HOUSE a trelliswork or wooden lath structure designed to give dappled shade and also to afford shelter from strong wind and a degree of protection from frost. They are mainly used in commercial nurseries but gardeners who specialize in bonsai often have them.

LATIN NAMES although Classical Latin died as an everyday language in the sixth century AD, Botanical Latin is a living language. Having survived the Middle Ages in its use by herbalists and doctors, its continued use was ensured by the immense work of the Swedish botanist, Carl Linnaeus, in the eighteenth century, who laid down the basis of the Latin **binomial system** used to name plants today. Botany is international and Latin makes it possible for enthusiastic gardeners to communicate with no other common language but the Latin names of plants. Even where gardeners do have a language in common, confusion would be widespread if we did not have the Latin names. For example, the flower called wake robin in America is *Trillium grandiflorum*, while in England this common name is used for *Arum maculatum*. Beginner gardeners should embrace Latin names from the start – they are not difficult. See **naming of plants**, **nomenclature**.

LAWN SAND a preparation for ridding lawns of broad-leaved weeds and mosses. It contains ammonium and iron sulphates and also promotes the growth of the grass.

LAYERING a method of propagation that involves rooting a shoot while it is still part of the parent plant. There are several layering methods, including **French layering**, but in simple layering you find a shoot that is near the ground and lower it so that it can be pegged down. You make a slit in the lower side and turn the tip of the shoot upwards, forming a more or less u-shaped bend. This is then buried so that the tip is above ground.

LAZY BED a **bed system** used for growing potatoes. Rather than planting them by digging, they are laid on the ground and soil is drawn over them. The drawing process is repeated as the shoots appear and are earthed-up.

It is a method that works in milder climates, where the shoots are not as vulnerable to frost and was very popular in Ireland, where the remains of lazy beds can often be seen beside abandoned cottages.

LEACHING the process by which any substance soluble in water, including soil minerals and plant nutrients, is washed downwards in the soil. The soil is then said to have been leached.

LEADER the shoot at the tip of the main stem of a tree or shrub.

LEAF-BUD CUTTING a **cutting** consisting of a leaf or part of a leaf along with its stalk and enough of the stem to include the bud in its **axil**.

LEAF CUTTING a **cutting** taken from a leaf or part of a leaf without an associated bud.

LEAF MINERS the **larvae** of several different kinds of insects tunnel through the leaves of a wide range of plants, eating out the fleshy inside part without disturbing the skin. The chrysanthemum leaf miner, for example, is a troublesome pest.

LEAF MOULD a term almost as widely misunderstood as **humus**.

LEAF CUTTINGS to propagate house plants require no specialist equipment.

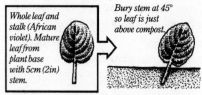

Whole leaf and stalk (African violet). Mature leaf from plant base with 5cm (2in) stem.

Bury stem at 45° so leaf is just above compost.

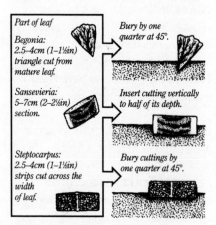

Part of leaf

Begonia: 2.5–4cm (1–1½in) triangle cut from mature leaf.

Bury by one quarter at 45°.

Sansevieria: 5–7cm (2–2½in) section.

Insert cutting vertically to half of its depth.

Steptocarpus: 2.5–4cm (1–1½in) strips cut across the width of leaf.

Bury cuttings by one quarter at 45°.

Leaf mould is not partly decayed leaves but a friable, dark, soil-like substance with a floury consistency, resulting from the near-complete breakdown of leaves. It is quite the best basis for potting composts for tricky plants and a magnificent soil conditioner.

LEAFLET one of the components of a compound leaf.

LEATHERJACKETS the **larvae** of the cranefly. They feed on roots and are a serious pest of lawns, causing the grass to die in patches.

LEG although a shrub technically has several stems arising at or near ground level, it can also be on a very short, single stem. This is called a leg, especially with reference to bush fruit.

LEGUME the seed vessel of pea-type plants, beans and so on, which are known as leguminous plants.

LEPIDOTE a term used to describe a plant or plant part covered with tiny scales. The leaves of some rhododendrons are lepidote.

LICHEN an organism consisting of a fungus and an alga whose tissues are intermingled and neither of which is parasitic. Lichens grow only in clean air on stones, walls or plants. They are not necessarily dangerous to the plants on which they grow, although they are usually thought to be.

LIGHT apart from the usual uses of the word, it also means the glazed component of a **cold frame**.

LIGNEOUS woody.

LIME strictly speaking, lime is the popular name for **calcium oxide** and **calcium hydroxide**. However, the term is loosely used in the garden to cover any substance that has the same general effect on soil.

LIME-HATER see **calcifuge, chlorosis.**

LINE OUT to plant out in rows young plants that you want to grow on before putting them in their permanent positions. You also line out **hardwood cuttings**.

LINEAR a term used to describe a slender leaf with the margins parallel or nearly so, but almost always coming to a point, e.g. a pine needle.

LINER (1) in the nursery trade a liner is a young plant in its first pot. Un-scrupulous retailers, of whom one may be thankful that there are few, will sell liners for prices approaching those of plants that are properly ready for planting out in the open garden.

LINER (2) material used to line a garden pond. See **pool liner.**

LIQUID FEEDING a method of feeding plants, mainly house plants but increasingly roses and other shrubs, by dissolving nutrients in the water with which they are irrigated. It is a routine

method, which **foliar feeding** should not be. It is expensive but clean, efficient and easily controlled.

LIQUID MANURE the original **liquid feed** and still the best. A sack, containing animal manure, is suspended in water for a couple of weeks and the resulting solution watered on to the plants.

LITTORAL a term used to describe plants and animals that live on the seashore. *Aubrieta* is a Mediter-ranean littoral.

LOAM a soil that is easily worked but nutritious and moisture-retentive.

LOGGIA another of those misused words like **patio**. It is a walk, usually from one building to another, only one side of which is covered-in. A gallery. It is *not* the same thing as a garden room.

LONG TOM an extra-deep plant pot, used primarily for plants with **tap roots**.

LOPPERS esssentially a pair of long-handled **secateurs**, but of more robust construction. Loppers are used to cut through thick wood that would be likely to damage secateurs.

MACRONUTRIENTS substances required by plants in quite large amounts. They can be remembered by the formula CHONSP (said as a word), which stands for for carbon, hydrogen, oxygen, nitrogen, sulphur and potassium. Calcium is also usually regarded as a macronutrient. See **micronutrients, NPK**.

MAIDEN a term used to describe a tree in its first year after grafting. Usually applied to fruit trees.

MALLET CUTTING a cutting consisting of a single leaf joint, with the leaf, **axillary** bud, and a short section of the stem. The stem section may be cut along its long axis. *Berberis* and *Mahonia* are propagated in this way.

MANGANESE one of the essential trace elements. It is needed for the manufacture of **chlorophyll** and symptoms of deficiency include yellowing between the leaf veins. It can be supplied quickly by the use of a foliar spray.

MANURE any material that contains nutrients that are available to plants. Manures include artificial fertilizers as well as animal manures, and there are also manures of plant origin, such as seaweed. The best all-round animal manure is from horses, with cow manure next best. Pig and poultry manure is usually much too high in nitrogen and is also 'cold', which means it does not perform well on heavy soils. You should not use animal manures when they are fresh, but leaving them in the open too long leads to their nitrogen being **leached**. Never apply animal manures and lime within three months of one another. The lime reacts with the nitrates with the formation of ammonia gas, which is given off to the atmosphere.

MARGINALS plants that grow best either in shallow water no more than a few centimetres deep or in soil that is permanently wet. They are planted at the margins of ponds or streams. A common marginal is marsh marigold (*Caltha palustris*).

MARGINATE a term used to describe a leaf with a distinct or conspicuous margin.

MARITIME a termed applied to seashore-dwelling plants or to gardens within about 10km (6 miles) of the sea, the limit of the drift of salt spray. A maritime climate is one that is influenced by the sea and therefore often relatively mild, as is the whole of Britain and Ireland.

MARL a **calcareous** clay added to sandy soils to make them more fertile and give them a better texture. Used more by groundsmen than gardeners.

MATTOCK also known as a cross-axe. An extremely useful tool that should be in many more garden sheds. It is like a short-bladed pick-axe but both tips are broadly chisel-shaped, the one fore and aft, the other side to side. It makes the job of removing stumps infinitely easier and is also ideal for breaking up hard or compacted soil.

MEAL in gardening, meal is the result of grinding a solid substance – bone-meal for example.

MEALYBUGS sap-sucking insects that protect themselves with a waxy, fibrous, powdery secretion. They can be serious pests in the greenhouse, attacking vines and many ornamental plants.

MEDIUM (1) used to describe anything in which plants are grown or propagated – soil, peat, coir, sand and so on.

MEDIUM (2) a term used to describe a soil that is neither heavy nor light.

MERISTEM a minute cluster of cells at the growing tip of a shoot. They are all-purpose cells that become differentiated into the various kinds of tissues.

MERISTEM CULTURE a form of **micropropagation** in which the meristem is used. It has the advantage of producing plants that are free of viruses and is a way of 'cleaning' up stocks.

MICROCLIMATE a term that is sometimes misunderstood. It applies to the climate of a specific and limited area such as a garden, part of a garden, or even the area around a particular plant or group of plants. Once you get to speak of a city or county, you should really refer to the 'local' climate, as you have gone beyond the bounds of 'micro'.

MICRONUTRIENTS the **trace elements**. See **macronutrients**.

MICROPROPAGATION a relatively modern development wherein plants are propagated from very small pieces of tissue in laboratory conditions. Plants that were hitherto difficult to propagate or hard to produce in commercial quantities are now in many cases readily available to gardeners as a result of micropropagation. We should not complain, however, if the costs of propagation are reflected in the prices.

MIDRIB the main vein of a leaf or leaflet. It usually runs down the

centre. In a **pinnate** leaf, although each leaflet has a midrib, it and its fellows arise from a **rachis**.

MILDEW a general fungal infection of damp materials, but in gardening there are mildews that kill plants. The most dangerous is the powdery mildew of rhododendrons.

MINERAL SOIL a soil in which there is less than 25 per cent organic matter. It will not make a good garden soil until large amounts of **bulky** manures have been added, along with more concentrated matter such as **leaf mould**.

MIST PROPAGATION the use of an automatically controlled, fine spray of water to keep the leaves of cuttings from wilting. Mist propagation units are available to amateur gardeners and are not very expensive, but they do need to be in a greenhouse. Because the cuttings in a mist propagation unit do not need to be covered over with plastic to maintain **humidity** and can thus be open to the air and light, rooting is much quicker than by other methods. Difficult cuttings such as camellias and conifers are rendered comparatively easy, and the whole business of propagating trees and shrubs in particular becomes very enjoyable indeed and highly productive.

MITES tiny, sap-sucking insects with four pairs of legs. The most prevalent of them is the red spider mite, which is almost invisible to the naked eye and is a pest in hot, dry conditions. It is not the same thing as the bright red, highly visible insect often seen running about harmlessly on paths and terraces. There are several kinds of red spider mite and between them they attack a wide range of plants. Risk of attack can be reduced by maintaining **humidity** around house plants and in greenhouses.

MIXED BORDER a **border** in which different kinds of plants – shrubs, herbaceous perennials, bulbs, even trees, all grow together. It is not quite as elementary as you might think and is in fact a recent 'concept' in gardening. There have been several claims to have 'invented' it, but the credit can be given quite reasonably to the thousands of home gardeners who have been applying common sense for generations.

MOLYBDENUM a **trace element**, necessary in the use of nitrates in plant tissues. Deficiency, which leads to distortion of leaves and growing tips, occurs on acid soils and can be corrected by liming.

MONOCARPIC a plant that dies after setting seed once.

MONOCOTYLEDON a plant that has only one seed leaf. Sometimes shortened to 'monocot'. See **cotyledon**, **dicotyledon**.

MONOECIOUS a term applied to a plant in which male and female flowers occur on the same plant. See **dioecious**.

MONOTYPIC a term used to describe a **genus** that has only one **species**, such as *Oxydendrum* and *Kalmiopsis*.

MORPHOLOGY the study of form. It is not, however, what you need in order to be a good bookmaker but the science of the development of living organisms.

MORTAR RUBBLE usually referred to as 'old' mortar rubble and frequently recommended in books on rock gardening for adding to the soil for certain plants that are reputed to need lime. Take no notice. It may be amusing to imagine the last old barn in Britain being torn down by a mob of desperate alpine gardeners, but most alpines will grow perfectly well with the addition of stone chippings. If you want to add lime, use limestone chippings, which are readily available from garden centres.

MOSS POLE, MOSS STICK a wooden pole covered with sphagnum moss used for supporting the sorts of house plants that climb and have aerial roots, such as Swiss cheese plant (*Monstera deliciosa*). An alternative method is to make a tube of plastic netting and fill it with damp sphagnum moss.

How to make a MOSS POLE for a monstera.

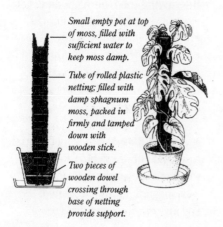

Small empty pot at top of moss, filled with sufficient water to keep moss damp.

Tube of rolled plastic netting; filled with damp sphagnum moss, packed in firmly and tamped down with wooden stick.

Two pieces of wooden dowel crossing through base of netting provide support.

MOUND LAYERING a method of propagation in which a plant is cut to the ground to allow new shoots to develop from the base. As the shoots appear, they are earthed-up so that they can form roots. Eventually they are detached as independent plants. It is used for blackcurrants and gooseberries as well as for several kinds of ornamental shrubs, such as *Philadelphus* and *Deutzia*.

MUCILAGE if you soak some seeds (such as those of the true acacias) in water – a good way of speeding up their germination – you will find a jelly-like substance left behind. This is mucilage.

MUCRONATE a term used to describe a leaf or bract that ends in an abrupt point.

MULCH a material added in the form of a layer to the surface of the soil. The most usual mulches are of organic matter – manure, peat, straw, composted bark, partly de-cayed leaves and so on. An organic mulch feeds the plants, suppresses weeds, reduces soil compaction, conserves moisture and helps to protect plant roots in winter. Artificial, non-organic mulches can be of plastic sheeting or mats (more widely used in forestry) and gravel,

MOUND LAYERING or 'stooling' (a) is an effective method of propagation for heathers and garden pinks. An alternative is dropping (b). Lift the plant and bury it deeper in the hole to encourage rooting.

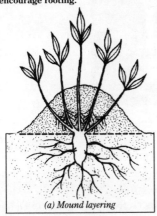

(a) Mound layering   *(b) Dropping*

which is valuable in alpine gardening for weed suppression, moisture conservation, keeping the vulnerable necks of the plants free from lingering wet, and preventing soil being splashed on to the leaves of the plants by rain.

MULE a sterile **hybrid**.

MUSHROOM COMPOST a compost made largely of horse manure, with chalk added. When it is 'spent' (finished with by the mushroom grower), it is a valuable material for adding to the soil as a conditioner or as a **mulch**. It is not a good idea, however, to use it on acid soils where rhododendrons and other **lime-haters** grow.

MYCELIUM the true 'body' of a fungus. The familiar toadstools and puffballs are the fruiting bodies of fungi. The organism itself consists of threads, called hyphae, and the mass of threads is a mycelium. A harmful fungus can never, therefore, be removed by simply destroying the fruiting bodies, you must get rid of the mycelium, which can be extremely difficult.

MYCOLOGY the study of fungi.

MYCORRHIZAL a term used to describe roots that associate intimately with the mycelia of beneficial fungi. Some plants with mycorrhizal roots need the presence of the fungus if they are to thrive or even germinate.

NAMING OF PLANTS as I have said elsewhere, it is important to get to grips with the Latin names for plants so that you can communicate without ambiguity with other gardeners from anywhere in the world. Once you have mastered the **binomial system**, you will start to find that snippets of useful information can also be gleaned from Latin names. Often a name will tell you something about the physical characteristics of a plant (*Ixia viridiflora* has green flowers) or about where it grows (*Myriophyllum aquaticum* is a water plant) or where it comes from (*Crinum asiaticum* comes from Asia). Sometimes it will tell you the name of the person who first collected it from the wild (*Pleione hookeriana*).

NATIONAL GROWMORE see **Growmore**.

NATIVE a term used to describe a plant that belongs to the natural **flora** and has not been introduced. Many 'wildflower' propagandists seem unaware of the distinction.

NATURALIZED a term applied to a plant has been introduced and subsequently become established in wild conditions. It is not native.

NECTARY a gland in a flower, producing nectar.

NEUTRAL SOIL a soil that is neither acid nor alkaline. Chemically, neutrality is expressed as a pH of 7, but most **lime-haters**, including rhododendrons (and azaleas) and camellias, need an acid soil with a pH of 5–6. One should bear in mind that a soil with a pH of 6 is ten times as acid as one with a pH of 7, and pH5 is 100 times more acid than pH7. See **pH**.

NICKING AND NOTCHING nicking is removing a sliver of bark just below a bud in order to stop it developing. Notching is the removal of a sliver of bark just above a bud to encourage it to grow.

NITRIFICATION the process whereby soil bacteria convert organic compounds of nitrogen, which cannot be taken up by plants, into available nitrates and nitrites.

NITROGEN FIXATION often confused with **nitrification**, nitrogen fixation is the process whereby certain bacteria and/or algae convert atmospheric nitrogen into compounds that plants can absorb. Such bacteria are to be found in the nodules on the roots of leguminous crops (including peas and beans), which is why you should cut such crops down, leaving the roots in the soil, rather than pull them up.

NO DIGGING a system of organic gardening in which the soil is never disturbed by digging but receives frequent, deep **mulches** of **bulky** organic matter. It is not recommended unless you are thoroughly experienced and able to discern and diagnose the things that can go wrong.

NODE the point on a stem where leaves, shoots or flowers arise. See **joint**.

NOMENCLATURE systems of naming organisms, designed to provide a world-wide, agreed standard. There are two codes that govern the naming of plants: the International Code of Botanical Nomenclature and the International Code of Nomenclature for Cultivated Plants. See **bionomial system**, **Latin names**, **naming of plants**.

NPK this stands for nitrogen, phosphorus, potassium (K being the chemical abbreviation for potassium). A fertilizer containing these three **macronutrients** may be labelled with their percentages by weight in the form '7-7-10', meaning 7 per cent nitrogen, 7 per cent phosphorus and 7 per cent potassium.

NURSERY a garden, commercial rather than private, where plants are propagated and grown on. A garden centre is usually not a nursery, as its plants are bought in from nurseries. A return of the specialized nursery as a major force in gardening is gathering momentum, and it is likely that the berberis-cotoneaster-conifers sameness of garden centre stock will become increasingly by-passed by a largely discerning gardening public.

NURSERY BED part of the home garden where young plants are grown on prior to being put in their permanent places.

NUT any hard, one-seeded, woody fruit that does not split open when ripe. An acorn, although never offered with the port, is still a nut. A peanut is not, but is defined by common sense rather than botany.

OB- a prefix meaning 'the other way round'. Thus a leaf that is obovate is egg-shaped but broadest above the middle; oblanceolate means lance-shaped but broadest above the middle; obconical means with the point of the cone at the lower end.

OBLIQUE a term used to describe the base of a leaf with the sides of different sizes and at different angles.

OFFSET a young plant growing alongside its parent and (usually) loosely attached to it. Offsets occur in bulbs, corms, many alpines and multi-crowned herbaceous perennials.

OPPOSITE see **alternate**.

ORBICULAR perfectly circular.

ORGANIC FERTILIZER generally a fertilizer derived from animal or plant remains or from the metabolism of living things. Examples of the former are hoof and horn, bone-meal, blood, fish and bone and seaweed meal. Urea is an example of the latter. See **inorganic fertilizer**.

ORGANIC GARDENING a highly sensible way of gardening in which emphasis is placed on making the soil not only fertile but also as perfectly structured as possible by the working-in of decayed organic matter. It tends to produce vegetables that taste bet-ter and plants that are healthier than those grown under a regime based mainly on **inorganic fertilizers**.

ORGANIC SOIL this is a soil with more than 25 per cent organic matter content.

OSMOSIS the movement of water across a membrane from solutions of lower concentration to those of higher concentration, as if to equalize the concentrations. Osmosis allows plants to take up water at the roots because the concentration of nutrient salts in the tissues is higher than that in the soil water. Since the membrane is semi-permeable it does not allow dissolved nutrients to flow in the reverse direction. If the soil is laden with chemical salts, the concentration may be higher than in the plant cells and water will flow out of the plant. This leads to wilting and death. Fertilizers are salts, and thus one result of over-fertilizing is to cause the plants to suffer from drought.

OSMUNDA FIBRE the chopped roots of the royal fern, *Osmunda regalis*. In Britain it is now little used, as the fern is a threatened species. In western parts of Ireland it is an extremely common plant but it would very soon become rare if exploited for orchid compost and use by florists.

OVERPOTTING potting-on into too large a pot. The roots do not occupy the new compost, which soon becomes waterlogged and sour.

OVERWATERING perhaps the commonest cause of failure with plants in pots. Too much water drives out oxygen and causes root death.

OVERWINTERING keeping plants going during winter that otherwise would die in a cold climate.

OXYGENATORS pond plants that grow under water and produce oxygen, which is dissolved in the water. It is important to include plenty of oxygenators in any garden pond to help keep the water clear. They compete with algae for mineral salts in the water and thus suppress algal growth.

PALMATE a term used to describe leaves shaped like a hand. The criteria are that there should be at least three lobes and they should originate from a common point. You should note that the **pinnate** fronds of a coconut palm are not palmate.

PANICLE a branched **inflor-escence**, each branch of which is a **raceme** or a **corymb**.

PANICULATE in the form of a panicle.

PARASITE a plant that obtains food from another and does harm to it, for example mistletoe (*Viscum album*).

PARTERRE strictly speaking, any level area of garden in which there are flower beds. It has come, however, to mean an area where the beds are geometrically or otherwise symmetrically arranged and is a type of **formal garden**. The word fundamentally means the same as **knot garden** but suggests something considerably larger, perhaps made up of several knots.

PATHOGEN a virus, bacterium or other micro-organism that causes disease.

PATIO originally, the inner courtyard of a Mediterranean-type house, with a pool, fountain and plants in containers in the moorish style. It is now applied to a paved sitting-out area next to a cold-climate house. This is also called a terrace.

PAVER a paving stone or flag (not the man who lays it).

PEAT partially decayed plant material, found in high-rainfall areas where few trees grow and a **hardpan** has formed. Peat derived partly from sphagnum mosses is harvested, milled and sold as moss peat and is an excellent medium for the gardener. It contains very little plant food but as it breaks down **humus** is formed and nutrients are released. Peat is a renewable resource, but it forms very slowly, at the rate of about 1m (3ft) every thousand years. British peat sources are small, but those in other countries, such as Ireland, are abundant and controlled extraction does not necessarily threaten its role as a natural habitat. Peat is a first-class **soil conditioner** and an unrivalled constituent of potting composts.

PEAT BED, PEAT GARDEN a raised bed, almost entirely filled with peat and often within walls made of **peat blocks**. There is no better structure in which to grow difficult acid-loving plants.

PEAT BLOCKS peat cut in blocks, dried but not milled. You can often buy dry blocks, but half-dried ones are best for making a **peat bed**. Peat cut for domestic fuel in Scotland, Ireland and elsewhere is in the form of blocks, and fuel blocks make fine peat walls if they are soaked in water before use.

PEAT POTS pots made of compressed peat, in which plants can be planted out without their roots being disturbed.

PECTINATE a term used to describe a part of a plant that looks like the teeth of a comb. The foliage of some conifers, such as the noble fir (*Abies nordmanniana*), is pectinate.

PEDICEL the stalk of an individual flower.

PEDUNCLE the stalk of an **inflorescence**.

PELLETED SEED seed coated with an inactive, soluble substance, sometimes containing an insecticidal or fungicidal dressing, so that it is in pellets, which are easier to handle.

PENDENT a term used to describe a part of a plant that is hanging, but not because of its weight (in which case it would be **dependent**) or because of weakness (**pendulous**). Something that is pendent is more hanging than 'nodding'.

PENDULOUS a term used to describe a part of a plant that is hanging because the part supporting it is too weak to keep it upright. See **pendent**.

PERENNIAL strictly, any plant that can live past two sets of seed (cf. **biennial, monocarpic**), but gardeners usually mean those that are not woody, which is to say herbaceous plants rather than trees, shrubs and also bulbs.

PERFOLIATE a term used to describe a leaf with united lobes that looks as though the stem passes through it. The **juvenile** leaves of the spinning gum (*Eucalyptus perriniana*) (known in the USA as the silver dollar tree) are perfoliate, as are the terminal leaves of the early cream honeysuckle (*Lonicera perfoliata*).

PERGOLA a framework of any material (brick or stone arches can constitute a pergola) up and over which plants can be encouraged to grow. The dictionary definition stipulates that there is a walk beneath it, but although this is usual, it is not necessary. What makes a pergola different from an arch is that it is in fact a succession of linked arches.

PERIANTH collectively, the **petals** and **sepals** of a flower. In bulbous plants, where the petals and sepals are not easy to tell apart, they are referred to as the perianth.

PERLITE expanded mica, added to potting composts for lightness and aeration. It is often recommended as a cuttings medium but I have always found it much less satisfactory than a simple peat/sand mixture.

PERMEABILITY OF SOIL the rate at which soil allows water to pass through.

PERPETUAL-FLOWERING a jargon phrase meaning that a plant flowers for a long time compared with similar ones. For example, perpetual-flowering roses bloom in Britain roughly from June to October, while the old-fashioned roses flower for about a month from mid-June. Perpetual carnations can be made to produce flowers all year round if various techniques are used but, although it may flower for a long time, each plant has its own season.

PEST any living agency bringing damage or disease to plants.

PESTICIDE any substance which, if applied to pests, kills them.

PETAL a modified leaf, one of the elements of the **corolla**.

PETALOID a term used to describe parts of a flower that have become like **petals**. Petaloid stamens (often known as petaloids) are of the same colour as the petals and may be anything from slender and strap shaped to something very close to the shape of the petals. Petaloid **sepals** are often indistinguishable from petals. Petaloid structures are involved in doubling. See **double**.

PETIOLE a leaf stalk. It is a good idea to become familiar with the terms **pedicel**, **peduncle** and **petiole**, as it is easy to confuse them with one another.

pH a measure of the acidity or alkalinity of a soil. The pH scale has values from 1 to 14, but is a logarithmic, not a simple progression. This means that each unit below the neutral point, which is 7, signifies a ten-fold increase in acidity, while each unit above 7 means a ten-fold increase in alkalinity. Thus, if your soil has a pH of 6 and your neighbours' garden soil registers 5, theirs is ten times more acid than yours. If yours is 7 and theirs is 5, your neighbours' garden is 100 times as acid. Simple pH test kits can be bought at any garden centre.

The degree of soil acidity or alkalinity, known as the **pH**, should be ascertained by carrying out a simple soil test.

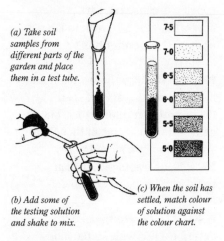

(a) Take soil samples from different parts of the garden and place them in a test tube.

(b) Add some of the testing solution and shake to mix.

(c) When the soil has settled, match colour of solution against the colour chart.

PHEROMONE TRAP a device for the control of certain insect pests such as **codling moth**. The traps consist of plastic triangular boxes containing a sheet of sticky paper and a capsule containing a pheromone – the substance the female moths use to attract their mates. The boxes are hung on the trees, the male moths are lured in and trapped on the sticky paper. Commercial growers use these traps to monitor pest numbers so that they can decide when to spray with insecticide.

PHLOEM plant tissue that conducts the products of **photosynthesis** from the leaves to other parts of the plant. It also helps to strengthen and support the plant.

PHOSPHORUS one of the three main elements essential to plant growth. It is used in the formation of the nuclei of cells and lack of it gives rise to very generalized symptoms of failure to thrive. See **macronutrients**, **NPK**.

PHOTOSYNTHESIS the process by which a plant, using the energy of the sun, converts carbon dioxide and water into complex organic molecules such as sugars, starch and cellulose.

PHOTOTROPISM the movement of a plant, including its growth, under the influence of light. See **heliotropic**.

PHYLLODE a modified leaf stalk (**petiole**), usually widened and flattened and superficially leaf-like, that has taken over the function of a leaf. Several *Acacia* species have phyllodes instead of leaves, and some, such as the blackwood acacia (*A. melanoxylon*), have a mixture of phyllodes and normal **pinnate** leaves.

PHYSIC GARDEN medicine was firmly founded on herbalism until quite recently in history, and the faculties of medicine of many universities in Britain and Europe had gardens attached to them in which the herbs could be grown and studied. These were the forerunners of the modern botanic gardens. The two best known English ones are at Oxford and Chelsea.

PHYSIOLOGY the study of how plants work, as opposed to **morphology**, which is the study of their form.

PICOTEE a flower with a band of contrasting colour round the edge of each petal. **Laced** pinks show a form of picotee edging.

PICTURESQUE in garden history, a movement in the eighteenth century that tried to make landscapes and gardens look like paintings by giving attention to texture and lighting. There was a also a rather nebulous romantic element.

PIN-EYED PRIMULA a primula flower in which the **style** is long and reaches or protrudes from the mouth of the flower. In a thrum-eyed primula the style is short and ends within the flower. Some primulas will not set seed unless flowers of both types are present.

PINCHING-OUT the process of removing the growing tip of a plant or of one of its stems by pinching with the fingers or finger and thumb. It makes the plant bushy by encouraging the formation of **side-shoots**.

PINETUM an **arboretum** devoted to conifers, not just pines.

PINNATE a term used to describe a compound leaf with a feather-like structure. Along the **rachis** there are two rows of more than three leaflets, called pinnae. In a bi-pinnate leaf the pinnae are themselves pinnate.

PINNATISECT a term applied to a leaf cut into deep divisions that are not individual leaflets. The leaf is divided, but not to the midrib, and the midrib is not a **rachis**.

PIPING a special type of cutting used for the propagation of pinks and carnations (*Dianthus*). The piping is made by pulling out the top of a young shoot without using a knife.

PISTIL the female organ of a flower, consisting of **stigma**, **style** and ovary.

PITCHER-SHAPED a term used to describe a bell-shaped flower that narrows at the mouth. Many of the Ericaceae (heather family) have such flowers. In practice, expressions such as this, including 'urn-shaped' and 'flagon-shaped' turn out to be vague and not really very helpful, as the vessels whose shapes they refer to are no longer seen outside museums.

PLANT BREEDER'S RIGHTS you may see this written against items in plant catalogues. It means that the plant concerned cannot be propagated for gain unless with the permission of the holder of the rights, who is then entitled to royalties on every plant sold.

PLANTLET an **offset**, but sometimes produced on leaves or stems.

PLANTSMAN OR WOMAN a person with a wide knowledge and appreciation of plants. It is a term of respect that cannot be applied by people to themselves but is, as it were, awarded. Plantsmen or women do not necessarily bother with the design effect of their plantings as long as the plants are happy, but some are excellent designers as well.

PLEACHING the process of plaiting branches together to make a screen. You will see pleached trees, particularly limes, as flat screens on either side of walks in large gardens that are open to the public. In the days when the country house was the centre of political intrigue, such walks afforded privacy and coolness for diplomats, princes and other rogues while they decided the fate of Europe.

PLICATE a term used to describe a leaf that is folded like a fan or pleated. A good example is the leaf of the popular shrub, *Viburnum plicatum*.

PLUG a small plant, grown in a compartment of a divided seed tray, which can be planted out virtually without disturbance. Summer bedding plants such as pelargoniums, fuchsias and lobelias are increasingly sold in spring as plugs.

PLUMOSE literally meaning 'feather-like', it is a term used to describe a plant part that is shaped more like a feather duster.

PLUNGE BED a bed, usually raised, consisting of a material into which pots can be sunk up to their rims. It can be outside or in a greenhouse and provides protection against frost and the drying out of earthenware pots as well as stability for taller plants in pots.

PODSOL an extremely acid soil that has been subject to severe leaching, usually with the formation of **hardpan**. Podsols are infertile and tend to be badly drained.

POLE-SAW a pruning saw on a long handle.

POLLARDING the process of cutting back all the branches in the head of a tree to the trunk. Pollarding is performed on street trees for the sake of space and on trees such as willows in order to create a spectacular display of coloured shoots after re-growth. Such trees are termed pollards.

POLLEN spore-like grains containing the male reproductive cells of a flowering plant.

POLLINATION the transfer of **pollen** from one flower to another, whether on the same plant or another. See **cross-pollination**.

POLLINATOR that which carries out pollination. It can be the wind; a fly, bee, wasp, beetle and so on; a bird, bat or rodent; or even a human being.

POLYCARBONATE a very lightweight, rigid plastic, used as a

Making a POOL with a plastic LINER.

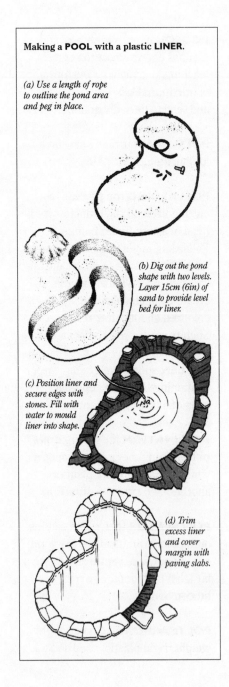

(a) Use a length of rope to outline the pond area and peg in place.

(b) Dig out the pond shape with two levels. Layer 15cm (6in) of sand to provide level bed for liner.

(c) Position liner and secure edges with stones. Fill with water to mould liner into shape.

(d) Trim excess liner and cover margin with paving slabs.

substitute for glass in greenhouses and conservatories.

POLYTHENE a lighter plastic than PVC and ideal as a glass substitute for **tunnels** and **cloches**. It is used in various forms as a weed suppressor, for propagation, and for protecting young plants.

POMPON a class of flowers, mainly dahlias and chrysanthemums, that are small, tight and ball-like.

POOL LINER any substance that will hold water and can be used as the base for a garden pool. Butyl rubber is currently the best but there are alternatives that are cheaper. See **PVC**.

POST-EMERGENCE WEED-KILLERS these act on weeds that have germinated. Pre-emergence weedkillers destroy weeds before they appear above ground.

POT-BOUND a term used to describe a plant whose pot has gone beyond the stage when it can be said to be full of roots. The roots will have become compressed and often twisted in a coil at the bottom of the pot. Some plants are said to flower best when 'slightly pot-bound'. What this means in practice is that you should not be too enthusiastic about potting them on but should also not let them become truly pot-bound.

POTAGER a vegetable garden laid out as a **parterre** or in a generally formal, ornamental way. It is not easy to make a convincing potager and few British examples work nearly as well as the many good ones in France.

POTASH see **potassium**.

POTASSIUM one of the three main elements essential to plant growth, also known as potash. Although vital, its precise functions are imperfectly understood but seem to have much to do with the adjustment of the plant to the prevailing conditions. Deficiency symptoms vary. See **macronutrients**, **NPK**.

POTASSIUM SULPHATE a highly efficient, concentrated potassium fertilizer that does not poison the soil in repeated applications, a fault of potassium chloride. The latter is also unsuitable for tomatoes, which have a high demand for potassium.

POTATO BLIGHT see **blight**.

POTTING-ON the process of moving a plant from one pot to another, larger, one. It is usually done when a plant is emerging from its dormant period or immediately after flowering. See **over-potting**.

PREPARED BULBS bulbs that have been treated to make them start growing quickly very shortly after being potted or planted in bowls. Hyacinths, for example, are prepared (forced) by producers so that, when potted in autumn, they flower in mid-winter.

PRICKING-OUT the process of transplanting very young seedlings from the seed tray or pot in which they have germinated into a larger vessel in which they are given more room to grow on. You can prick seedlings out into individual pots or put several in a larger pot, or you can use a box (known as a 'flat') for larger quantities. The term is also applied to **cuttings**.

PROCUMBENT the term used to describe a stem that lies along the ground but without making roots.

PROPAGATING the process of increasing plants by seed or by **vegetative** means. For many people the best part of gardening.

PROPAGATING CASE often known as a propagator, this is in effect a miniature **greenhouse**. The most usual type sold to home gardeners consists of a large plastic seed tray on which sits a transparent plastic dome. A heated propagator has the tray mounted above a heating device with a thermostat. Propagating cases can be used for any method of propagation except hardwood cuttings and layering and are a good investment.

PROPAGATING FRAME the only practical difference between this and any other kind of **frame** is that it is made to be as airtight as possible in order to maintain a humid atmosphere. Otherwise, any frame you successfully use for propagating is a propagating frame.

PROPAGATING HOUSE a greenhouse which is used solely for propagating. It usually contains a **mist propagation** unit and **propagating frames**.

PROPAGATOR see **propagating case**.

PROPAGULE a piece of a plant – from a shoot to a few cells – used for propagating.

PROTECTED CULTIVATION the practice of growing plants under cover.

PROTECTION providing the means, not necessarily in the form of covering, whereby plants can be grown in conditions in which, if they were not protected, they would be likely to die. A **mulch**, for example, is as much a form of protection as a **cloche**.

PROTHALLUS one of the two generations of a fern; a very small, scale-like structure which arises from a spore and carries the male and female cells that unite to form the fern plant as we recognize it.

PROTOPLASM the contents of a living cell.

PRUINOSE a term used to describe a plant part that is thickly covered with white **bloom** (i.e. a waxy-powdery coating).

PRUNING the process of cutting back woody plants. Cutting down herbaceous perennials is not pruning. Pruning is one of the things in gardening that needs the most study and understanding, but the most important lesson of all to learn is: 'When in doubt, don't prune'. The old gardeners will tell you that 'Nothing ever came out of a book', but the best way to learn pruning is to look it up and then remember it.

PRUNING TOOLS secateurs, loppers, long-handled pruner, pole-saw, pruning saw, pruning knife. The first two are essential, even for a beginner at gardening.

PSEUDOBULB the prefix pseud- means 'looks like but isn't'; hence a pseudobulb is a storage organ that looks like a bulb but is not a bulb. Many kinds of orchids, including pleiones, arise from pseudobulbs.

PTERIDOPHYTES ferns and their close relatives.

PUBESCENT literally 'becoming hairy', a term used to describe a plant part that is covered with fine, soft hairs.

PUNGENT not sharp-smelling in this context, but a term applied to

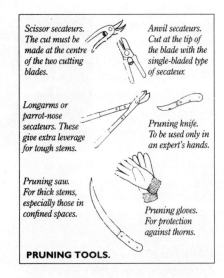

Scissor secateurs. The cut must be made at the centre of the two cutting blades.

Anvil secateurs. Cut at the tip of the blade with the single-bladed type of secateur.

Longarms or parrot-nose secateurs. These give extra leverage for tough stems.

Pruning knife. To be used only in an expert's hands.

Pruning saw. For thick stems, especially those in confined spaces.

Pruning gloves. For protection against thorns.

PRUNING TOOLS.

sharply pointed leaves, specifically those with a very long point of almost needle-like sharpness, as in some yuccas.

PVC (POLYVINYLCHLORIDE) a tough plastic, used as sheeting. It acts as a substitute for glass, as a weed suppressor and as a cheap form of **pool liner**. Black or semi-transparent versions are available.

PYRAMID a term used to describe certain forms of fruit trees.

QUAD- a prefix denoting four or four-fold, as in quadrangular, meaning four-angled.

QUIESCENT a term applied to a seed that cannot germinate because conditions are unfavourable. If the conditions are favourable for germination and a living seed will not germinate, it is said to be **dormant**.

RACEME an unbranched, usually elongated **inflorescence**, in which each flower has its own stalk.

RACHIS the main axis of a compound leaf.

RADICAL a term applied to leaves that arise directly from the root.

RADICLE the embryonic root of a plant; the first organ to advance into the soil after germination.

RAISED BED strictly speaking, a **bed** is a raised bed if the soil level is above the general level of the garden, but in common-sense gardening parlance it is a bed, raised above the general level, whose sides are supported. The support can be from sleepers, logs or other arrangements of wood; **peat blocks**, or walls made of any suitable material.

The uses of raised beds are much more important than how they are constructed. They can be used to provide improved drainage and sometimes, when made so that they can be covered at any particular season, to provide **protection**. A raised bed can contain soil entirely different from that of the surrounding garden so that, for example, **lime-haters** can be grown where the general soil is **calcareous**. It can also raise small alpines to a level where they can be appreciated without stooping or kneeling.

Raised beds are ideal for disabled gardeners, who can work them from wheelchairs, excellent for blind people, who can follow the wall round while enjoying the scents and textures of the plants, and can incorporate seats and several other types of features, including water-courses and **bubble fountains**.

RAKE unless well-made and looked after properly, a rake will be short-lived. Spring-tines rakes, perfect for raking leaves and lawn debris, are notorious for breaking and you should always buy the best you can afford.

RAY FLORET, RAY FLOWER a small flower with a petal that is tubular at first and then flattened. Usually appearing as a ring round a cluster of **disc** florets in a daisy-type flower.

REJUVENATION the process of pruning the old branch framework of a fruit tree to encourage a mass of new growth, from which a new framework can be created.

REMONTANT a term applied to plants that flower more than once a year. It is used particularly when comparing the flowering of modern roses with the once-flowering old-fashioned types or the ramblers. It is also applied to strawberries.

RENEWAL PRUNING (1) the practice of pruning apples and pears so that a constant supply of young growths is produced.

RENEWAL PRUNING (2) the practice of pruning ornamental shrubs hard so that many more new growths are made than would be otherwise. It is carried out when a shrub becomes leggy or top-heavy, but it cannot be done on shrubs that do not tolerate being pruned into old wood. The pineapple broom (*Cytisus battandieri*) responds well to this type of renewal pruning.

RENEWAL PRUNING (3) the practice of pruning old shoots out at ground level to encourage strong, new, flowering shoots from low down in the bush. This is the best way to prune hydrangeas, for instance.

RENIFORM a term used to describe leaves that are kidney-shaped.

REPOTTING some gardeners who love pedantry more than accuracy distinguish between repotting and potting-on. There is no difference. Those who say that repotting is the act of putting a plant into a different pot of the same size are attempting to split non-existent hairs.

RESISTANCE some plants have a natural immunity to a disease. They are said to be resistant to it. Plant breeders have made great strides in recent years in producing resistant varieties of some garden plants. If your plants tend to suffer from a particular disease, such as **rust**, it makes sense to seek out and grow resistant varieties.

RESPIRATION it may be surprising to non-botanical people to learn that plants respire. This does not mean that they have lungs; respiration in plants is an internal process of breakdown of plant foods, accompanied by the release of energy.

RETARDING the deliberate delaying of plant growth by any means – chemical, mechanical or by the use of light and temperature.

RETICULATE a term used to describe a leaf or other plant part that is 'netted' or furnished with a network of veins (e.g. the leaves of *Salix reticulata*), fibres (as in the skins of corms) or colouring. The petals of *Camellia* x *williamsii* 'Donation' are reticulate in veining and also in colouring, as the veins are a darker pink than the background.

REVERSION (1) the process whereby a plant that is different from the wild type returns wholly or in part to the original. It happens frequently with variegated plants, such as variegated forms of box elder (*Acer negundo*) and Norway maple (notably *Acer platanoides* 'Drummondii'). Reverted shoots (in these cases green) should be removed as soon as they are seen to halt the process.

REVERSION (2) a disease of blackcurrants in which the leaves become smaller and cropping is badly reduced. It is thought that the bushes are reverting to the wild type, but whether this is true or not, the disease is spread by the big-bud mite. See **big bud**.

RHIZOME a specialized stem, which may run under the soil or along its surface, producing shoots at nodes along its length and at its tip. Well-known rhizomatous plants include bearded irises and couch grass (twitch, scutch). Rhizomes of many garden plants can be cut for propagation.

RING-BARKING see **girdling**.

RING CULTURE a system of growing greenhouse crops, chiefly tomatoes. The plants are grown in bottomless pots (rings) containing a nutrient compost, set on gravel. Only the gravel is watered, while liquid feeds are applied to the compost. Ring culture is now fast

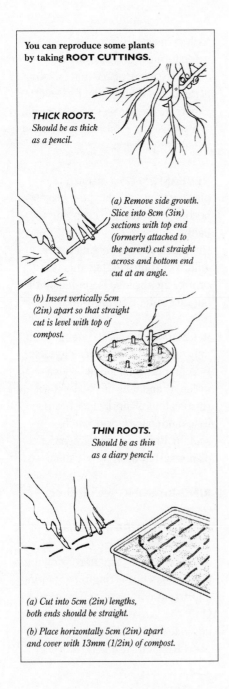

You can reproduce some plants by taking **ROOT CUTTINGS**.

THICK ROOTS.
Should be as thick as a pencil.

(a) Remove side growth. Slice into 8cm (3in) sections with top end (formerly attached to the parent) cut straight across and bottom end cut at an angle.

(b) Insert vertically 5cm (2in) apart so that straight cut is level with top of compost.

THIN ROOTS.
Should be as thin as a diary pencil.

(a) Cut into 5cm (2in) lengths, both ends should be straight.

(b) Place horizontally 5cm (2in) apart and cover with 13mm (1/2in) of compost.

becoming out of date as other methods, particularly the use of **growing bags** and pots containing soil-less compost, become more popular, even among professionals. These systems come into their own where the soil is not very good or infected with disease, or where there is no soil at all, as in a courtyard or even roof garden.

RIPE a term used to describe the wood of a tree or shrub that is fully mature and hard.

ROCK GARDEN a better term than 'rockery'. A rock garden, when properly built, becomes a home-from-home for alpine plants and looks natural. A rockery is really a heap of rocks.

ROCK PHOSPHATE finely ground, phosphate-bearing rock, sold as a slow-release fertilizer. It is very variable and some samples have half the amount of usable phosphate of others.

ROCK PLANT any plant suitable for the rock garden. See **alpine**.

ROGUEING the process of separating undesirable plants from those you want to keep. For example, when you sow seed of the shell-pink

Primula pulverulenta 'Bartley Strain', a few of the seedlings will have flowers with the normal red colour of the species. These seedlings should be rogued out before they can set seed to increase the purity of the strain.

ROOT BALL the roots of a container-grown plant and the soil around them.

ROOT CUTTINGS pieces of root, usually removed during the dormant season and rooted by burying them shallowly in a cuttings compost. Some plants, such as *Geranium cinereum* 'Ballerina', *Arnebia pulchra* (the prophet flower) and *Papaver orientale* (Oriental poppy) are best propagated by this means, which gives you an excuse to leave the Christmas festivities before the fights start!

ROOT HAIRS tiny hairs on the roots, just one cell thick, through which the plant absorbs water and inorganic salts. They are invisible to the naked eye and not the same thing as the hairy roots that are readily to be seen.

ROOT PRUNING the process of cutting right through several of the roots of a tree to make it grow less

vigorously and put its energy into fruiting. It is also one of the techniques used in **bonsai**.

ROOT RESTRICTION the **root run** of a plant can be restricted, contained within a barrier, to induce it to fruit, as with figs, or to keep it within bounds, as with culinary mint.

ROOT RUN the extent of the roots of one plant or the actual soil invaded by them. It can be cool (as under a rock), moist (as anywhere in Ireland), extensive (as in well-cultivated, deep soil), restricted (see **root restriction**), shallow, and so on.

ROOTING HORMONES substances in powder or liquid form used to assist in the rooting of cuttings. Used wrongly or carelessly, or on plants that are unsuited to their use, rooting hormones can actually retard rooting. If used sparingly just on difficult subjects and not liberally used as a catch-all, they are a boon.

ROOTSTOCK a plant grown specially to supply the roots to a grafted plant – or any plant on to which a **scion** is grafted or budded.

ROSE the perforated bulb at the end of a hose or watering can. Do not buy just one rose: about three, including a very fine one for watering seedlings, a coarse one for watering among shrubs, and a medium rose for general use, will be a good investment.

ROTATION the practice of changing the positions of crops in the vegetable garden to avoid growing the same crops on the same piece of ground in consecutive years. It reduces the chance of disease organisms building up and makes best use of the soil, some plants preferring freshly manured ground, while others prefer soil from which a crop has been taken.

RUDIMENTARY a term used to describe any plant part that is not properly formed.

RUGOSE a term used to describe a leaf that is wrinkled and deeply veined, as in *Rosa rugosa*.

RUN-OFF rain that is allowed to run away over the soil. It is bad practice to permit any run-off, as it washes away valuable soil and undermines plants. In rock gardens, tilt the stones backwards, to give retaining walls a backwards **batter** and make shallow soakaways alongside paths.

RUNNER a stem that grows along the soil surface, producing roots and new plantlets at intervals. Eventually, the stem itself dies and the plantlets form new, independent plants. Strawberries reproduce using runners.

RUST a number of fungal diseases produce rust-coloured spots on leaves and stems. They tend to weaken plants and are difficult to control. Mint, roses, hollyhocks, antirrhinums and chrysanthemums all have their own rusts. **Resistant** varieties are available.

SAGITTATE a term used to describe an arrow-shaped leaf.

SAMARA a winged seed, such as those of maples and ashes. I expect you thought it was a Russian car.

SANDSTONE a type of rock that is highly suitable for rock-garden building because it contains no lime and hence the widest possible range of plants can be grown in association with it.

SAP the fluid in the tissues of a plant. It is a very complicated substance in composition. Gardeners should be wary of the sap of all plants, even if they think they know them well. Many kinds of irritant and even poisonous materials are present in the saps of many plants. For example, euphorbia sap can cause temporary blindness if you allow it to touch your eyes, the sap of hellebores can strip the skin from your hands, and that of oleanders kills, even if only a tiny amount is ingested.

SAPLING any young tree before its inner **heartwood** hardens enough to support it against major stresses.

SAPWOOD the tissue surrounding the **heartwood** of a tree or shrub through which nutrients and water are actively transported.

SAXICOLE a plant that grows on or among rocks. Saxifrages are saxicoles.

SCAB not a healing reaction to superficial injury as in animals, but a surface roughening caused by disease.

SAXIFRAGES.

Saxifraga cochlearis

Saxifraga 'Hindhead Seedling'

SCALD see **sun scald**.

SCALE INSECTS small, brown, limpet-like insects often found on the backs of the leaves of house plants and greenhouse plants. They do a lot of damage and should be dealt with promptly.

SCANDENT a term used to describe a plant with climbing stems.

SCAPE any erect flower stalk, arising from near the ground and having no leaves. However, it may have **bracts** which, if enclosing the flower cluster, are called spathes. A good example of a spathe is found in the arum lily (*Zantedeschia*

aethiopica). In this type of arrangement the part of the scape within the bract is termed the **spadix**.

SCARIFY (1) to use a rake or scarifier (a toothed metal tool) to pull moss and grass 'thatch' (dead material below the grass blades) from a lawn.

SCARIFY (2) to overcome the resistance of hard seed coats to taking in water by chipping, abrading, or treating with an acid. Acid treatment is not recommended for use by home gardeners.

SCHIST a kind of rock made up of layers that split apart readily. It is not suitable for rock-garden building because the layers are certain to split apart under the action of frost.

SCION part of a plant – a shoot or bud – cut away and grafted on to a **rootstock**.

SCOOPING AND SCORING methods of propagating bulbs. Scooping consists of scooping out the basal plate of the bulb, while in scoring you make cuts in it. Either action stimulates the production of **bulblets**, which can be grown on to become bulbs.

SCORCH dry, brown patches on leaves due to the action of strong sunlight, wind, salt spray, inappropriate use of fertilizers, or disease. If water is allowed to lie on the leaves of greenhouse plants in full sun, the droplets sometimes magnify the rays of the sun, leading to scorch marks. See **sun scald**.

SCRAMBLING PLANT in gardening the distinction is made between a climber, which grows upwards by clinging, using tendrils, suckers, aerial roots or twining stems, and scramblers, which gain height by thrusting long branches into and through shrubs and trees, often assisted by having prickles. Rambling roses are scramblers.

SCREE many people think, incorrectly, that scree is the correct term for a **top dressing** of pebbles on rock gardens. In fact a scree must be constructed correctly with sufficient depth, with graded stones (the largest at the bottom) and with a small amount of humus-rich soil. Plants that have very long root systems in nature that are difficult to grow in the ordinary rock garden will thrive in a scree garden.

SCYTHE nowadays superseded by the **strimmer** but mentioned here because it is a dangerous implement in inexperienced hands. Do not buy one unless you are young and fit and have a very strong back.

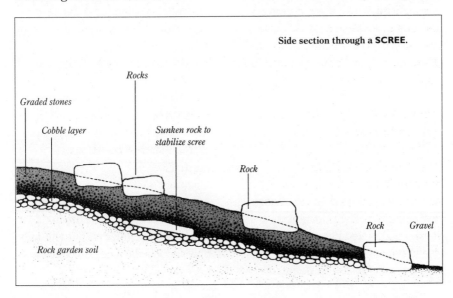

Side section through a **SCREE**.

Rocks

Graded stones

Cobble layer

Sunken rock to stabilize scree

Rock

Rock garden soil

Rock

Gravel

SECATEURS for pruning.

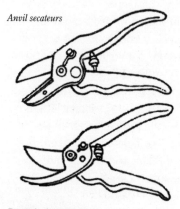

Anvil secateurs

Parrot-beak secateurs

SECATEURS (pronounced secat-urze, not secat-ears). Shears for pruning, designed to be held in and used by one hand. There are three main types: parrot-beak, bypass and anvil. Parrot-beak secateurs have a scissors action; in the bypass type a sharp blade passes close to a broad blade; and in anvil secateurs the upper, sharp blade cuts on to the flat ridge of the one below it. Secateurs will damage plants if they are not kept properly sharp or if you try to cut shoots that are too thick.

SEDGE PEAT peat formed in what are, in effect, recently formed bogs, containing a high proportion of sedges and reeds. It is not a very useful type of peat, as it disintegrates quickly and is ineffective as a potting medium. The British deposits are small and should be preserved. See **peat**.

SEED DRESSING a pesticide applied to seed so that it is attacked neither as seed nor as just-germinated seedlings.

SEED VIABILITY if a seed can germinate, it is said to be viable. Viability in general is the ability to develop. Many seeds remain viable only for short spells of time, a problem that faced the plant hunters before air travel, when a Himalayan primula, for example, might have lost its viability before it reached a port in India, let alone Britain or America. The viability of seeds is prolonged if they are kept cool and dry.

SEEP HOSE plastic hose with a row of tiny holes through which water seeps in a form of **trickle irrigation**. This applies water just where it is needed and is a good system where water is scarce for any reason.

SELECTIVE WEEDKILLERS weedkillers that can be applied to the general vegetation but will kill only the weeds. They are often used on lawns.

SELF-COLOURED a term used to describe flowers of one colour.

SELF-COMPATIBLE a term applied to fruit trees that are capable of self-fertilization. The opposite is self-incompatible.

SELF-STERILE a term used to describe a plant that cannot set viable seed after being pollinated with its own pollen.

SEMI-DOUBLE a term applied to a flower that has just a few more petals than the normal wild species. See **double**.

SEMI-RIPE CUTTINGS these cuttings are neither soft nor fully mature. This is the best state in which to take summer cuttings of woody plants. As a guide, a semi-ripe cutting can be thought of as one that is too firm to bend more than thirty degrees from the vertical but which will not crack as it approaches that angle.

SEPAL one of the segments of the outer part of the flower or **calyx**. The sepals enclose and protect the (usually) softer parts of the flower within the bud and are often hidden by petals when the flower opens. Nothing is that simple, however, and sepals are often modified, sometimes becoming indistinguishable from petals.

SERRATE a term used to describe a leaf with saw-like teeth.

SESSILE a term used to describe any plant part that is stalkless or very nearly so.

SETS small bulbs, ready for planting, of onions and shallots. They cut out the time and space necessary to grow these crops from seed. The term is also sometimes applied to potato tubers.

SETTS cubical or brick-shaped stones, used for ornamental paths.

SEXUAL PROPAGATION the process of growing plants from seeds or spores. Exciting, but not in the way you thought.

SHADING everyone with a conservatory, greenhouse or cold frame comes up against the need for shading in summer. Proprietory slatted blinds are excellent, shading the glass not just the inside of the house, but they are relatively expensive. White greenhouse shade paint is very good but needs to be removed in autumn. Plastic shade netting, cut and tailored to the individual greenhouse or frame, is inexpensive, handy and, if properly anchored, highly efficient and reasonably attractive.

SHELTER BELT see **belt.**

SHODDY the waste from woollen mills, traditionally used as a nitrogenous fertilizer, but unreliable and not recommended these days.

SHOOT (1) the first top-growth made by a plant as it germinates.

SHOOT (2) a growth of the current year.

SHORT-DAY PLANT one that will only flower when the light it receives drops below a certain total amount per day. Chrysanthemums and poinsettias are short-day plants.

SHREDDER a machine that chops up woody material so that it can be used as a mulch or added to the compost heap. It needs to be used with great care.

SHRUB not a scientific word. Shrub is a loose term for a woody plant with several shoots arising at or near ground level rather than a single distinct trunk. Forms of the

popular *Magnolia* x *soulangiana*, for example, are so often sold as shrubs that eminent horticulturists have been known to argue that they are not trees. In fact, kept to a single stem, many of them make extremely noble trees of 20m (65ft) or so.

SHRUBBERY people do not talk much these days of a shrubbery, but rather of a shrub border. 'Shrubbery' became an item in the repertoire of comedians and was rapidly thought of as vulgar. 'Shrub border' sounds grander, but I suspect that, as the **mixed border** becomes even more widely recognized as one of the best ways to grow plants, the term 'shrub border' will decline in use.

SHRUBLET again a loose term, meaning a very small or dwarf **shrub.**

SHY-FLOWERING a term used to describe a plant that will flower in its due season but very sparingly.

SIDE-SHOOT a shoot arising from the stem below the apex.

SIDE-SHOOTING rubbing out or otherwise removing side-shoots. Side-shooting is used in tomato culture.

SILICA silicon dioxide, the mineral that makes up sand and quartz and is present in clays. The stems of bamboos are strengthened with silica and any bamboo litter should be left to decay and not be cleared up, as it will return silica to the soil.

SILT a soil with very small particles, usually deposited after suspension in water. Silts are excellent as far as fertility goes but very tricky to work with, as they are impossible when wet and very prone to **capping**.

SILVICULTURE the management and culture of woodlands, especially for commerce. One aspect of silviculture that is slowly returning is the production of 'round wood', which, if it catches on widely, will greatly assist the establishment of wild life. Round wood consists of straight, young branches, used for certain types of furniture.

SINGLE if a flower has the normal number of petals, i.e. the same as the species in the wild, it is said to be single, any more, and it is semi-double. If it has a lot more it is **double**.

SINGLING the process of removing seedlings to leave single ones at the required intervals. A form of **thinning**.

SLIP a slightly old-fashioned word for a **cutting**, but one that is still widely used.

SLOW-RELEASE FERTILIZER a fertilizer that releases its nutrients over a long period. Also known as controlled-release fertilizer. Most organic fertilizers release their nutrients slowly as they are broken down by bacteria.

SLUGS slugs and snails are the bane of a gardener's life. Many people do not wish to use chemical control, especially pellets, which may harm birds and other wildlife. Numerous alternative methods of control are recommended from beer traps to crushed egg-shells and from electric 'fences' to simply collecting them up after dark with torch and plastic bag. Possibly the best way is to encourage garden birds, although your efforts will be for nothing if you also keep a cat.

SLURRY if a farmer offers you a load of farmyard manure, make sure it is well-rotted, strawy material and not slurry. Slurry is an evil-smelling, anti-social liquid that has no place in the home garden.

SNAG a small stump left after bad pruning, natural damage or taking cuttings. Snags usually die back and provide points of entry for disease and should always be removed or preferably not allowed to occur.

SOD see **turf**.

SOFT FRUITS fruits that grow on canes or bushes, including strawberries, as opposed to top fruits, which grow in trees. Note that the opposite is not 'hard' fruits.

SOFT WATER any water that contains only small quantities of dissolved minerals. Rain water is soft. Water that contains large amounts of minerals, particularly calcium compounds, is said to be 'hard' and is not as suitable for watering plants as soft water, although its disadvantages have been greatly exaggerated.

SOFTWOOD timber from conifers. See **hardwood**.

SOFTWOOD CUTTINGS these **cuttings** are taken before the shoots have started to turn woody.

SOIL CONDITIONER anything that improves the structure of the soil. In the past, the term has tended to be reserved for materials such as sand, grit, lime and so on, but more recently has become used for organic materials such as manures and peat, perhaps the best soil conditioners of all.

SOIL MARK (NURSERY MARK) the abrupt change in colour at the base of a stem, usually quite noticeable and indicating the soil level where the plant grew before being lifted. You should always try to plant so that the nursery mark is level with the soil in its new location.

SOIL STERILIZATION when sowing minute seeds or spores of plants that take a long time to develop, they are likely to be overcome by mosses, liverworts, bracken sporelings and any pests or their eggs present in the soil. The soil can be sterilized by heat or by using a chemical. At home, if just one or two pots of soil need to be sterilized, you can cut a disc of filter paper to fit the surface of the soil and then pour boiling water through the compost. It is best to use a clay pot or one made of heat-resistant plastic. Do not remove the paper until you sow, and then keep the pot covered with a piece of clean glass. This method works well for ferns.

SOIL STRUCTURE this is determined by the way in which soil particles clump together to form crumbs with pore spaces between them.

SOIL TEXTURE not the same thing as soil structure, but the relative amounts of sand, silt and clay particles and their sizes. These give the soil its feel and appearance – hence texture.

SOIL-LESS CULTIVATION growing plants without soil, as in **hydroponics**.

SOUR soil that is low in oxygen because of waterlogging or extreme acidity is said to be sour.

SPADIX the fleshy axis of a flower spike often surrounded by a spathe. See **scape**.

SPAWN the **mycelium** of mushrooms: what you 'sow' when growing them.

SPECIES the rank immediately below **genus**. The name of a plant is its species name, consisting of the genus name, which comes first, followed by the species (specific) epithet. Thus, *Camellia japonica* is the name of the species and denotes that the plant belongs to the genus *Camellia*, specifically the species *C. japonica*. See **binomial system, Latin names, naming of plants**.

SPECIMEN (1) a plant at the peak of condition and approaching maturity or a plant, usually a tree or shrub of striking or noble appearance, planted in isolation to show off its form and have the maximum impact.

SPECIMEN (2) just another word for a plant, as in 'a poor specimen' or 'a well-grown specimen', and so on.

SPHAGNUM PEAT moss **peat** in which a high proportion is derived from sphagnum moss.

SPIKE an unbranched **inflorescence** on which the flowers have no stalks.

SPIKING the process of aerating the lawn by driving a fork into it or using a special spiking tool.

SPILING a method used by growers of show vegetables to obtain the longest possible roots on carrots and parsnips. A hole is driven deeply with a crowbar and filled with fine, rich, usually somewhat sandy soil into which a seed is sown.

SPINE a sharp, stiff point on a leaf or branch.

SPIT the depth of a spade or a trench the depth of a spade.

SPORANGIUM a body containing **spores**, as seen on the backs of fern fronds.

SPORE a reproductive cell that becomes a new plant without having to meet another.

SPORT a change in structure, leaf form, leaf or flower colour on part of a plant as a result (usually) of a natural process. Sports can be propagated **vegetatively** and become **cultivars**.

SPRAY a group of flowers on a stem.

SPUD besides being a slang word for a potato, a spud is any small digging or weeding tool with a narrow blade.

SPUR (1) a very short branchlet with whorls of leaves and clusters of fruit buds. Spurs can branch to form multiple spurs.

SPUR (2) a sac-like protrusion in the corolla of a flower, usually pointing backwards like the spur on a riding boot. You will see spurs in *Diascia* and *Aquilegia* flowers, for example.

STAG-HEADED a term applied to a tree badly affected by disease, old age or sometimes acid rain, with branch ends bare of leaves and branchlets and even, in extreme cases, of bark. Although it is characteristic of the damage caused by **acid rain**, do not rush into that diagnosis without checking out other possibilities such as a change in the water table.

STAGING the benching in a greenhouse or at a flower show.

STAKING the provision of a support for a newly planted tree by

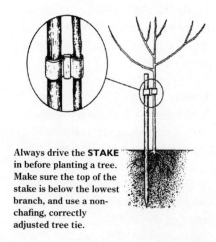

Always drive the **STAKE** in before planting a tree. Make sure the top of the stake is below the lowest branch, and use a non-chafing, correctly adjusted tree tie.

means of a stake driven well into the ground to which the stem is attached by a proper **tree tie**. The use of lash-ups involving discarded pantie-hose, old inner tubes and the sleeves of manky pullovers is poor gardening and damages the trees, as well as providing proof positive that you are a cheapskate. Nowadays various systems of short staking are preferred to the traditional long stake. Staking is also used for tall-growing perennials, in which case canes and garden twine are used.

STAMEN the whole of the male organ of a flower, consisting of **anther** and **filament** and bearing **pollen**.

STAMINODE a **petaloid** stamen.

STANDARD (1) the upper petal in pea-type flowers and the erect petal(s) of an iris flower.

STANDARD (2) a shrub grown on a stem longer than it would have if left to grow naturally and usually with its head at a predetermined height. Fuchsias, roses, bay trees and many other shrubs, including wisterias, are grown as standards.

STEEPING (1) soaking seeds in water before sowing.

STEEPING (2) preparing **liquid manure**.

STIGMA the tip of the female organ (**pistil**) of a plant, where pollen is deposited.

STIPULE a small **bract** at the base of a leaf stalk.

STOCK PLANT a plant kept and grown specifically for the production of propagating material, whether seed or material for **vegetative** methods.

STOLON a prostrate stem that roots and produces plantlets at the tip and sometimes at the nodes.

STOMATA the pores, mainly on the undersides of leaves, through which a plant 'breathes'.

STONE FRUITS peaches, apricots, nectarines, plums, damsons and cherries.

STOOL a plant that has been cut back to make it produce many new shoots from the base. This is done to make material for propagation (deciduous azaleas, chrysanthemums, etc.) or sometimes for decorative effects, as with *Eucalyptus* and *Paulownia tomentosa*. The process is known as stooling.

STOPPING the process of removing the growing tip to encourage side growths. See **pinching-out**.

STOVE HOUSE a greenhouse kept at about 21°C (70°F) in winter, in which tropical plants are grown. An expensive business. Also known as a hot house.

STRAINING BOLT a device, often called a wire strainer, for keeping wire on tension, usually used for support wires on walls but also for those that support **espaliers** and **cordons** in the open.

STRATIFICATION originally, the practice of putting seed between layers (strata) of sand in a cold place to break its dormancy. Now applied to various dodges, including putting the pots of sown seed or the seed mixed with damp sand or peat, into the domestic refrigerator. This practice has not yet been documented as a cause of marital dispute but you can bet it sometimes is.

STRATUM rock gardening books will tell you that the rocks should be laid in strata. Strata is the plural of stratum, a layer. In nature, most rocks except certain volcanic ones are in more or less horizontal layers, usually fractured and fissured, and if you are building a rock garden you should try to follow the pattern.

STRAW home gardeners seldom realize what a good buy a few bales of straw are. Bought in late summer, they are ideal for protecting young plants and groups of plants in pots. If you pick them up in early spring and stack them somewhere out of the way, they will rot down to make a superb compost for mulching and soil conditioning.

STRAWBERRY POT a tall pot with holes in the sides through which strawberries or ornamental plants can grow.

STRESS it is fashionable nowadays to complain of stress, but did you realize that it applies to plants as well? Any adverse conditions set up stress in a plant – cold winds, drought, overwatering, too much fertilizer and too few nutrients are among them. Prolonged stress kills plants and even short, stressful periods will prevent a young plant from ever reaching its full potential.

STRIKE to succeed in rooting a cutting. Gardeners speaking of 'a good strike', 'a poor strike', ' a hundred per cent strike' are not recounting the success of picketing but of propagation. It was said of a famous nurseryman that 'he could strike the spokes of an old umbrella'.

STRIMMER a spinning head, armed with nylon cord or other cutting attachments, driven by electricity or petrol; used with a scything motion to clear weeds.

STUMPERY a rather bizarre feature of Victorian gardens, in which trees were cut down to leave substantial stumps, among and even on which ferns and generally sombre plants were planted.

STYLE the long part of the **pistil** between the **stigma** and the ovary.

SUBEROSE corky.

SUBSHRUB a plant with stems that are woody for part of their length and herbaceous for the rest. It may be described as a perennial with a woody base and non-woody shoots.

SUBSOIL the soil lying underneath the **topsoil**. The fertile soil in which cultivation can be carried out is surprisingly shallow, often only one **spit** deep and sometimes less. Beneath it is the subsoil. This is infertile, relatively airless and of a poor structure, containing little in the way of organic matter. Furthermore, mineral salts that have been **leached** downwards will collect in the subsoil in forms that are unavailable to plants and may, in fact, be poisonous to them. Subsoil should never be mixed with the topsoil, but it is a good idea to break up the subsoil by **double digging**. Make sure that this is carried out correctly and that the subsoil is not dragged up into the top spit.

SUBSOILING a deeper version of **double digging**, with the aim of improving drainage. It is usually done on an agricultural scale, but if you find yourself with a deep **hardpan** you will have to think about subsoiling.

SUBSTRATE whatever a plant can grow in or on. As well as soil, it can be compost, water, sand, wood, rock and so on.

SUCCESSIONAL a term used in the special sense of sowing at intervals to give a succession of flowering or cropping.

SUCCULENT (*NOUN*) a plant that stores water in specially adapted, fleshy leaves or stems. You will often read of 'cacti and succulents'. The fact is that cacti are succulents but a non-scientific convention saves 'succulent' for succulents other than cacti. Yes, I know, but if you read this again it will become a little more clear.

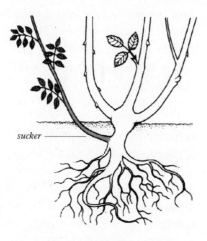

Removing a **SUCKER** (identified as emanating from *below* position of propagation).

SUCKER not the victim of a rogue garden centre but a shoot arising from the parts of a plant that are below ground. Suckers on grafted or budded plants should be removed as soon as possible and from as low down as possible, otherwise they may take over completely and your original rose or lilac will be lost.

SULPHATE OF... an old-fashioned way of referring to certain chemical compounds of sulphur. Ammonium sulphate, for example, is known as sulphate of ammonia.

SULPHUR it surprises many laymen that sulphur should be one of the **macronutrients** for plants, but it is vital to the making of **chlorophyll** and without it the leaves turn yellow and death follows. It is also a major component of many **enzymes** that govern plant growth. Powdered sulphur is an excellent fungicide.

SUN SCALD damage to leaves and shoots caused by exposure of shade-loving plants to sunlight, the action of sunlight through glass, or strong sunlight on very young plants. It is popular myth that watering the garden in sunlight causes scald. Indeed, it does not. Were it to do so, then every shower of cold rain on a sunny spring or summer day would cause scald spots, a circumstance suggesting that plant life could not have evolved in the first place and that none of us would be here to debate the subject anyway.

SUPERPHOSPHATE a fertilizer formed by treating **rock phosphate** with sulphuric acid to increase its phosphate proportion by dissolving away other fractions. The process also makes it soluble in water so that it can be made part of a liquid fertilizer.

SWAN-NECKED HOE a type of **draw hoe** with a pronounced curve in its neck.

SWARD a stretch of grass. A lawn. The word implies green-ness and richness of growth.

SWOE the brand name of a most excellent hoe with an offset neck attached to one end of a three-edged blade that can be used forwards, backwards and sideways. It is virtually indestructible.

SYMBIOSIS the intimate association of two organisms to their mutual benefit. A **lichen** is an example of symbiosis. This is different from parasitism, in which one of the organisms is harmed, often fatally. However, in symbiosis divorce is not an option.

SYNERGISM sometimes, the combined effect of two substances used together is greater than the sum of their effects when used separately. This is known as synergism and it often occurs with garden chemicals. Always obey the instructions when dealing with chemicals, especially the ones that say 'do not use this material in conjunction with...'.

SYNONYM an alternative name for a plant. When two botanical names for a plant are current, one is generally more accepted by botanical authority than the other, which is relegated to the status of synonym. For example, *Lithospermum diffusum* is (unless it has changed between my writing this and your reading it) the synonym of *Lithodora diffusa*. Some decades ago the situation with the name of this plant was the other way round. Gardeners feel some frustration at the apparent vagaries of plant **nomenclature** and who can blame them? See **Latin names, naming of plants**.

SYSTEMIC a term used to describe herbicides, pesticides and fungicides that are absorbed by a plant and spread throughout its tissues. A systemic insecticide, for example, makes any part of the plant lethal to a sap-sucking insect. See **contact insecticide**.

TANG the slender metal extension of the head of a tool such as a trowel that is inserted into the handle.

TAP ROOT a long, deep, strong, main root, sometimes swollen as a food reserve, as in carrots. Tap-rooted plants are often impossible to move safely once they are established.

TARSONEMID MITES a large group of very small mites. They attack strawberries, cyclamen and a wide range of greenhouse and house plants, causing distortion of leaves and flower buds.

TAXON any group of plants placed in a botanical category, such as a **genus, species** and so on.

TAXONOMIST a scientist who seeks to put nature into categories.

Taxonomists live on shifting sands but are for ever seeking firm ground.

TENDER a term applied to plants liable to injury or to die if grown outside in frost-prone areas. As with **hardiness**, it is a relative term.

TEPAL a segment of a **perianth** in which it is not possible to tell petals from **sepals**. Lilies and clematis have tepals.

TERMINAL a term applied to any plant part that grows at the tip of a stem.

TERRACE originally a flat area separated from its surroundings by being raised on one or more sides. In addition it now means a flat area with some degree of formality, as when paved, and usually separated from the rest of the garden by a low wall or a balustrade.

TERRARIUM much the same as a **Wardian case**.

TESSELLATED a term used to describe petals of leaves with a chequered pattern. The flower of the snake's head fritillary (*Fritillaria meleagris*) is tessellated, and there is a distinct group of tessellated colchicums.

THATCH the greyish-brown detritus beneath the surface of a lawn.

THINNING the process of reducing the number of plants to bring their number and spacing down to what you require. Seed of vegetable crops subject to infestation with flies (carrotfly, for example), should be sown thinly in the first place, as thinning attracts the insects.

THONGS the thick, fleshy roots of plants such as Asiatic gentians and seakale.

THRIPS commonly known as 'thunderflies', thrips are very small insects with rasping mouthparts. The most damaging in temperate regions are the greenhouse thrips, which attack many

different kinds of plants, and the onion thrips, which are by no means confined to onions but attack a great many plants both outdoors and indoors.

THROAT the deep part of a flower, often differently coloured from the rest.

THRUM-EYED PRIMULA see **pin-eyed primula**.

THUNDERFLIES see **thrips**.

TILTH a fine, crumbly soil suitable for seed sowing. Often referred to as a 'fine tilth'.

TINE a prong of a fork.

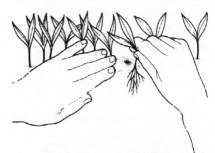

THINNING. Hold the seedling you want to keep in place with one hand while removing unwanted plants with the other.

TIP-BEARER a fruit tree that bears fruits at the tips of its shoots. Clearly, tip-bearers need special pruning in order to avoid removing all the fruit buds.

TIP-LAYERING a method of propagation used for blackberries and their allies.

TOMENTOSE a term used to describe leaves, shoots or fruits that are covered with woolly hairs.

TOP DRESSING anything put on the soil surface over the rooting area of a plant is a top dressing. It can be a quick-acting fertilizer, forest bark, garden compost, peat, leaf mould, pebbles and so on.

TOP FRUIT fruit borne on trees, as distinct from **soft fruit**.

TOPIARY the ancient art of clipping and/or training trees and shrubs into shapes. They can be purely geometrical, entirely abstract, or can depict animals, birds or even more way-out things such as ocean liners, steam engines and cars.

TOPSOIL the layer of fertile soil above the **subsoil**.

TORTRIX MOTHS a large group of moths whose caterpillars attack about as many kinds of plants as you can think of, from strawberries to oaks.

TOXIN a poison produced by a living organism, usually used to denote a substance made by a disease organism but also used for the **alkaloids** produced by plants such as oleander.

TRACE ELEMENTS chemical substances that are essential to plant growth but only in very small quantities. Also known as **micronutrients**. Among them are manganese, zinc, boron, molybdenum, iron and copper. Deficiency of any trace element will cause poor growth. See **macronutrients**.

TRANSLOCATION the movement of water within a plant, along with whatever is dissolved in it, including **systemic** substances.

TRANSPIRATION the loss of water vapour from plant surfaces, mainly from leaves and chiefly through open pores called **stomata**.

TRANSPLANT (1) (VERB) to move a plant from where it is planted to another position.

TRANSPLANT (2) (*NOUN*) a young plant that is about to be or is ready to be transplanted.

TREE a woody plant with a single main stem, branching some distance from the ground. See **shrub**.

TREE GUARD any metal, plastic or wooden structure or device put around a tree to protect it from animals and machines.

TREE PRUNER a very long-handled tool with a device at the end for pruning, one blade of which is worked by a lever operating a stiff wire. Of all the garden tools I have ever used, I found this the most maddening and the least efficient.

TREE SURGEON a practitioner of tree surgery. He or she must be an athlete, adept at climbing and must combine self-discipline of a very high order with a cool, calculating brain and a deep knowledge of Murphy's law. The tree surgeon must also be an artist with an eye for symmetry and beauty. Tree surgeons examine, diagnose and treat trees as well as removing dead and diseased wood and can also **head back** a tree of any size while preserving its proportion. Tree surgeons who do not charge highly enough for their time are likely to be charlatans, and few charge too much. Gardeners are ill-advised to try to do their own tree surgery at anything above ladder height, and those who use a ladder must be extremely careful. The chief tool a tree surgeon uses is a chain saw, an item that is not recommended for amateur use.

TREE TIE a device for securing the stem of a newly planted tree to its stake. Modern tree ties are plastic straps, furnished with spacers, that keep the stem away from the stake and prevent chafing. They can also be adjusted as the stem increases in diameter. It should be a routine task to go round the tree ties and make sure they are properly adjusted and have not slipped, especially after strong winds. Infamous substitutes such as nylon stockings are not recommended. See **staking**.

TRELLIS a framework of crisscrossing wooden laths, making a network of diamonds or squares used to support climbers and other wall plants.

TRENCHING a step further than **double digging**. The soil is dug to three **spits** deep with the removal of the top two. The third spit is broken up where it lies. It is a good way of

breaking up **hardpan** but is not prac-
tised much in gardens these days.

TRICKLE IRRIGATION a method
of watering the garden using
various devices that allow water to
be delivered precisely where it is
wanted. It is very economical but
also efficient. See **seep hose**.

TRICKLE TAPE a flat version of a
seep hose.

TRIFOLIATE with three leaves.

TRIFOLIOLATE with three leaflets.

TRIPARTITE a term used to
describe a plant part that is divided
into three almost to the base.

TROMPE L'OEIL literally 'to deceive
the eye', a technique used in garden
design which aims to alter our percep-
tion of what is actually there. It can
involve mirrors and such things as
gates, perspectives and distant views
painted on walls. False perspective, in
which for example the distances
between objects (trees, shrubs and so
on) in a row are graded to make the
rows seem longer, or leading a path
beyond a hedge so that it appears to
go further than it really does, are a
couple of the ways in which we can
make our small gardens seem larger.

TROPISM a tendency of a plant or
part of a plant to move in a specific
direction in relation to an aspect of
the environment such as light
(**phototropism**), gravity (**geotropism**) and the sun (**heliotropism**).

TROUGH GARDEN a garden made
in an old stone sink or drinking
trough. Since nearly all such vessels
have been bought up for the purpose
or command ludicrous prices, they
are often made satisfactorily with a
mixture of sand, peat and cement
with chicken-wire reinforcement.
Trough gardens will often support
tricky alpines that will not grow well
in the open rock garden.

TRUE plants are said to 'come true'
from seed if they are similar to their
parents. One of the problems with
the current definition of a **cultivar**
is that it is very difficult for amateur
gardeners to know which plants with
cultivar names can be grown 'true'
from seed and which cannot, e.g.
Viola 'Cuty' comes true from seed
but *Viola* 'Irish Molly' does not.

TRUG a shallow, oblong basket for
collecting cut flowers or vegetables.

TRUMPET narcissus flowers have
a **perianth** and a corona, which is the
inner, forward-facing development

that looks like a cup. Indeed, when the latter is shorter than the outer perianth segments it is called a cup. If the corona is as long as or longer than the segments of the outer perianth it is known as a trumpet and such narcissus are grouped as trumpet narcissus. The plural of narcissus, by the way, is narcissus, but gardeners usually say 'narcissi'.

TRUNCATE a term used to describe a plant part that is as if cut short, like the apparent upper lobe of the leaf of *Liriodendron tulipifera*.

TRUNK the main stem of a tree once it has grown beyond the sapling stage.

TRUSS a cluster of flowers, arising from a single centre and of more or less compact structure. The term is used especially for rhododendrons and tomatoes.

TUBER a swollen root or stem, usually underground. Potatoes are tubers.

TUBEROUS a term applied to a plant that has tubers.

TUFA a very soft rock consisting of an aggregate of petrified plant material. It is highly porous and it

is quite easy to plant small alpines directly into it. Difficult plants will often grow on tufa when other methods fail.

TUNIC a loose, dry skin round a bulb or corm. It can be papery or fibrous and is part of the plant, not rubbish to be removed.

TUNNEL (POLYTUNNEL) a form of greenhouse consisting of plastic sheeting drawn tightly over metal hoops. Shade netting can be used instead of the usual **polythene**.

TURF grass in general, but specifically squares of grass for laying as a lawn. In Ireland turf is the word for peat. In the USA turf is known as sod and there are sod farms many square kilometres in area.

TURFING IRON a spade-like tool with an ace-of-spades head and a strongly curved **tang**, used for lifting **turf**.

TWIG a general term for a small, woody branch.

TWINER a plant that climbs by twining its stems around a supporting structure, a tree or a shrub. Runner beans and bindweed are both twiners.

UMBEL a flat-topped, umbrella-shaped **inflorescence** such as that of cow parsley (*Anthriscus sylvestris*).

UNARMED without spines.

UREA an organic chemical occurring in animal urine. It is a high (45 per cent) nitrogen fertilizer that can be used as a top dressing or in solution as a foliar feed. Urea can be and mostly is made synthetically for use in gardens.

URN properly a vessel shaped like the funeral urns of the Roman Empire, but now used loosely (as is everything else classical) to refer to any earthenware garden container, usually in the phrase 'urns and tubs'.

VALVE one of the parts into which a seed vessel splits.

VARIEGATED a term used to describe a plant part, usually a leaf, that is margined, striped, splashed, spotted or zoned with a different colour or colours to the normal one.

VARIETAL the adjective derived from '**variety**', as in 'varietal differences'.

VARIETY botanically a category below species. A variety differs slightly in its botanical structure from the norm and is given its own name following 'var'. For example, *Myrtus communis* var. *tarentina* is variety of common myrtle with white fruits rather than the normal purple-black. See also **cultivar**.

VASCULAR SYSTEM the tubes or vessels in a plant through which food and water are conducted.

VASE, VASE-SHAPED a term usually applied to a plant with an open, depressed centre.

VEGETATIVE BUD a non-flowering bud.

VEGETATIVE PROPAGATION a method of increasing plants by means other than seed, including cuttings, grafting, budding, layering and division.

VEIN a bundle of conducting tissue visible from the surface of the stem, leaf or petal.

VELUTINOUS velvety (why don't they say so?).

VENATION the way in which **veins** are arranged.

VENTILATOR a window or louvre in a greenhouse. Always order twice as many as the manufacturer normally supplies.

VERMICULITE a very light, mica-based material similar to **perlite**.

VERNAL a term meaning of or appearing in spring.

VERNALIZATION the process of breaking the dormancy of seeds in order to speed up germination. It also applies, chiefly in commercial horticulture, to bulbs and other plants. See **stratification**.

VIABILITY a term used to describe the capacity of seed to germinate. It depends on conditions, and while some seeds can remain alive for a thousand years, the viability of others can be measured in days.

VINE EYE (1) a broad, triangular nail with a hole through which a wire can be threaded. Vine eyes are used for attaching wires to a wall and keeping them at a short distance from it. They should be used with a **straining bolt**.

VINE EYE (2) a short length of stem of a grape vine with one bud on it, used for propagation.

VINE WEEVILS see **weevils**.

VIRUS a non-cellular parasite consisting of a central molecule of nucleic acid surrounded by protein molecules. Viruses multiply inside living cells, using up their protein and causing disease. There are many problems in plants associated with viruses and most of them are incurable and best prevented by good garden hygiene.

VITICULTURE the practice of growing grape vines.

WALK a word used in large gardens for 'path'.

WALL NAIL a very hard nail for driving into walls but with a very soft head (usually lead) that can be bent round a wire.

WALL PLANT any plant that can be grown against or trained on a wall. Also a plant that can be planted in a wall, such as house leeks (Sempervivum).

WARDIAN CASE a glass case that is completely enclosed and airtight. Plants can grow in it because a recycling system builds up that is self-regulating. It was used to transport plants over long distances, and Dr Nathaniel Ward successfully despatched plants to Australia in his first examples in 1833. Wardian cases revolutionized plant collecting. The same principle is used in **bottle gardens**, **terraria** and **propagating cases**.

WARM HOUSE the same thing as a hot house! Also known as a **stove house**. The point is that subtropical plants and others from relatively frost-free places will thrive in a **cool house**, but a collection of plants more **tender** than that is almost certain to include some that need much higher winter temperatures.

WATER GARDEN a water feature in or alongside which moisture or water-loving plants are grown.

WATER SHOOT a very vigorous, vertical shoot growing from the upper surface of the branch of a

A **WATER GARDEN** can be as unpretentious as a lined wooden tub filled with water and planted with dwarf plants.

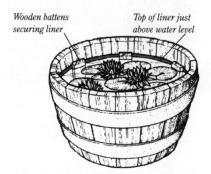

Wooden battens securing liner

Top of liner just above water level

tree or shrub. Seen on fruit trees, often after overenthusiatic pruning, and on slightly tender trees and shrubs when recovering from being cut back by severe frost. They are unproductive and should be cut off at the base.

WEANING the process of removing rooted cuttings from the rooting environment to a more open one.

WEED a plant in the wrong place.

WEEVILS amazingly, the weevils are the largest family in the Animal Kingdom. However, only one, the vine weevil, is likely to be a real nuisance and then by no means in every garden. The best way to be without them is to keep all warm,

dry places (greenhouses, frames and so on) scrupulously clean and tidy.

WETTABLE POWDER a powdered pesticide that will not dissolve in water but which forms a suspension evenly throughout a body of water, as in a watering can.

WETTING AGENT a substance such as washing-up liquid, added to another to make it cling better to a surface. For example, the systemic weedkiller 'Roundup' is most effective in killing bindweed if it is first mixed with washing-up liquid. It will then be absorbed and carried right down to the roots.

WHETSTONE a stone used for sharpening tools.

WHIP a very young tree with no side growths.

WHITEFLIES very common, tiny, white, moth-like insects that attack a range of different plants, especially under glass. They can be controlled by spraying or by **biological control**.

WHORL three or more plant organs attached at the same **node**.

WILD GARDEN a garden that resembles nature – not just a

parochial version of nature, but as world-wide as the inventory of garden plants allows. This is not the same as a 'wild-flower garden' which is confined to the native flora of the country in which it is situated. A wild garden may include hardy geraniums from Britain, meconopsis and primulas from the Himalaya, gunneras from Chile and astilbes from Japan if conditions allow, all growing naturally and taking care of themselves with minimal interference.

WILTING the loss of fluid pressure in a plant, leading to drooping and sometimes death. Many gardeners imagine that wilting is always caused by lack of water in the soil, but it is not necessarily so. It is the lack of water in the plant that causes wilting. This may be a result of root damage, overfertilizing or disease or even overwatering.

WIND-ROCK root damage caused by the plant moving in the wind. **Staking** combats it.

WIND-THROW the uprooting of trees by wind, as seen in the UK after the great gales of 1987 and 1990. It is not the same as **windfall** (1).

WINDBREAK anything, from a sheet of plastic or a fence to a belt of shrubs, that breaks the force of the wind.

WINDFALL (1) tree branches blown down by wind.

WINDFALL (2) a ripe or nearly ripe fruit that has fallen to the ground.

WIRE STRAINER see **straining bolt**.

WOOD ASH a useful fertilizer, rich in potash and **trace elements**, which should be applied when fresh. You should clear away the ashes of bonfires, as they can raise the **pH** of the soil at the site so high that little will grow.

WOODLAND GARDEN traditionally the planting of garden plants among trees and originally the conversion of existing woodland to garden by planting in it and then thinning the trees out. In the modern sense of the word a woodland garden can be made in the environment created by the planting of just two or three trees and a few shrubs or even under one deciduous tree.

WOODLICE also called slaters, these creatures, whose nearest relatives are shrimps, live in and digest decayed plant material of all sorts.

They are basically beneficial but will eat small seedlings under glass if you do not maintain proper hygiene.

WOUND DRESSINGS paints and other substances applied to wood that has been cut or damaged, to protect it from insects or disease. The practice of painting the cut stumps where branches have been removed is now recognized as useless, but some tree surgeons feel they must do it lest the customer thinks they are not doing the job properly. Emulsion paint from the penny bazaar is as effective or ineffective as many an expensive concoction but it no doubt encourages customers to settle their bills.

WOUNDING the process of removing a sliver of bark from the base of a cutting to encourage rooting. There does not seem to be any published proof of its effectiveness.

XEROPHYTE a plant adapted to living in conditions of extreme dryness or one that has evolved to avoid the effects of periodic or prolonged drought.

XYLEM a type of conducting and supporting tissue in which water and nutrients are transported upward from the roots.

YARD the name used in the USA for a garden at the back of a dwelling house.

YIELD how much of a crop you obtain from a given area.

ZEN GARDEN one of the styles of Japanese garden, developed in the courtyards of the Zen temples during the sixteenth century. The creation of a Zen garden is a minimalist art, barely gardening at all in the sense of cultivation, but intensely spiritual, depending on quiet, contemplative creativity in the raking of the sand which is its main component.

ZINC one of the **trace elements**. It is necessary for enzyme formation and deficiency shows itself in poor leaf development, such as 'little leaf' in citrus and peaches.

ZYGOMORPHIC a term that is used to describe a plant part that is bilaterally symmetrical, or symmetrical along one plane only. For example, the flower of a deciduous azalea is zygomorphic; the right and left halves are symmetrical but the upper and lower ones are not.